MW00339619

Touching the Breath of Gaia

Other titles by Marko Pogačnik

published by Findhorn Press:

Nature Spirits & Elemental Beings

Healing the Heart of the Earth

Earth Changes, Human Destiny

Christ Power & the Earth Goddess

The Daughter of Gaia

published by Lindisfarne Books:

Turned Upside Down

How Wide the Heart *(with Ana Pogačnik)*

Touching the Breath of Gaia

59 Foundation Stones for a Peaceful Civilization

Marko Pogačnik

Translated by Tony Mitton

© Marko Pogačnik 2007

The right of Marko Pogačnik to be identified as the author
of this work has been asserted by him in accordance with
the Copyright, Designs and Patents Act 1998.

First published by Findhorn Press 2007

ISBN 978-1-84409-097-6

All rights reserved. The contents of this book may not be reproduced
in any form, except for short extracts for quotation or review,
without the written permission of the publisher.

British Library Cataloguing-in-Publication Data.
A catalogue record for this book is available from the British Library.

Translated and edited by Tony Mitton
Illustrations © Marko Pogačnik 2007
Cover design by Damian Keenan
Layout by Thierry Bogliolo
Printed by WS Bookwell, Finland

1 2 3 4 5 6 7 8 9 10 11 12 13 12 11 10 09 08 07

Published by
Findhorn Press
305A The Park,
Findhorn, Forres
Scotland IV36 3TE

Tel 01309 690582
Fax 01309 690036
email: info@findhornpress.com
www.findhornpress.com

Contents

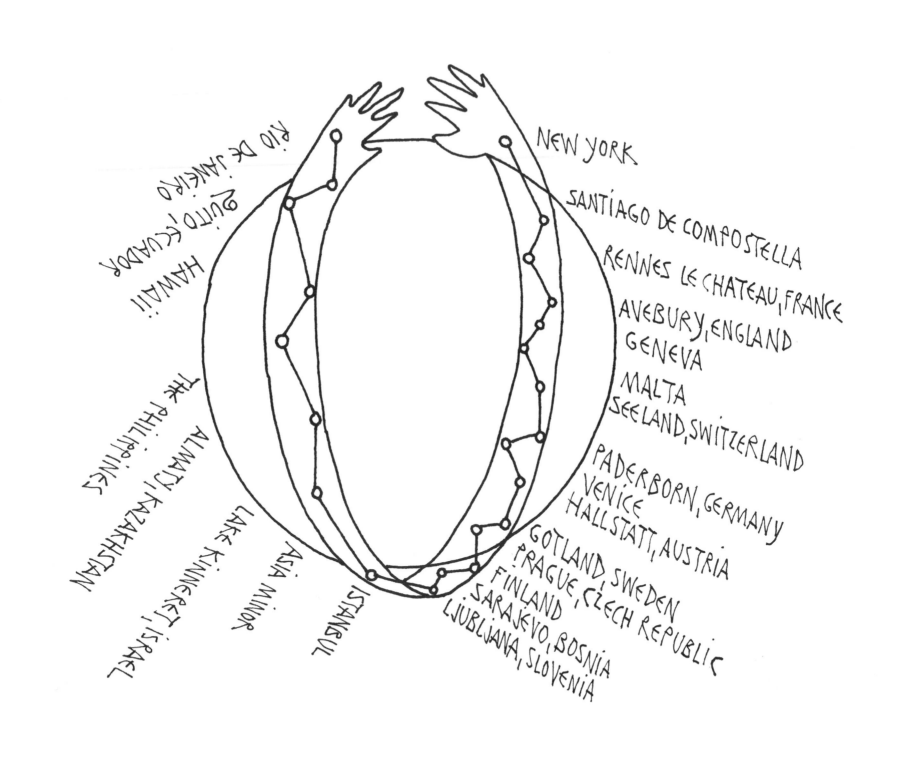

RIO DE JANEIRO
QUITO, ECUADOR
HAWAII
THE PHILIPPINES
ALMATY, KAZAKHSTAN
LAKE KINNERET, ISRAEL
ASIA MINOR
ISTANBUL

NEW YORK
SANTIAGO DE COMPOSTELLA
RENNES LE CHATEAU, FRANCE
AVEBURY, ENGLAND
GENEVA
MALTA
SEELAND, SWITZERLAND
PADERBORN, GERMANY
VENICE
HALLSTATT, AUSTRIA
GOTLAND SWEDEN
PRAGUE, CZECH REPUBLIC
FINLAND
SARAJEVO, BOSNIA
LJUBLJANA, SLOVENIA

The girdle of love and reverence that is laid around the earth.

6

The book before you was conceived as a living dialogue with the Earth Soul. The language used belongs to the consciousness of Earth, first expressed through non-logical natural apparitions such as crop circles, and here creatively reshaped and finally applied to tell Earth of our love. One would like to tell her about our visions for a new and peaceful civilization that is the goal of an increasing number of people from the most various cultures – a civilization that would be unthinkable without communicating with the consciousness of Earth.

For the past three years I have been travelling round the world engaged on a variety of earth acupuncture projects that are linked to my artistic activities and geomantic research. Based on this experience, I have chosen the places and landscapes, 23 in number, which form the book's basic pattern. However, this is not a travelogue but rather it is a serious attempt to enter into conversation with the earth as a whole – actually, to resume communication with the Earth Soul.

I am aware that all over the world many people have a burning interest in experiencing the earth holistically and developing affectionate, creative relationships with her Being. Our alienation from the Earth Cosmos hinders this endeavour: I observe this alienation as derived from our civilization's orientation towards intellect. The present book is structured in practical fashion to help rebuild one's personal and collective relationship with the wholeness of Earth. This is why it is conceived as an interactive instrument

Note first that the book contains 23 full-page black-and-white structural drawings that serve as vital-energetic fields. They are designed to resonate with different qualities of Earth Consciousness. Their role is to enable the Earth Consciousness to resonate its presence in the book. Its presence is made directly possible by these 'energetic drawings' whose construction follows the principle that Nature abhors a vacuum. Art historians have falsely applied this concept, translated as a 'fear of emptiness', to the way in which the art of primitive peoples treats expansive surfaces. Children and primitive people tend to fill in any given surface completely, leaving no space empty. This is not about fear. Quite the opposite, the practice represents a celebration of life's abundance and the completeness of the Earth Cosmos, in which small children and primitive people still participate. Drawings based on the principle of Nature's abhorrence of a vacuum accord with the holistic character of the consciousness of Earth and Nature, which penetrates the whole of life and ensouls each of its individual particles.

This brings us to the 59 chapters that comprise the body of the book. Of these, 23 chapters are devoted to the places and land-scapes that anchor the girdle of love and reverence that is laid around the earth. The girdle begins in New York, runs across Europe, Asia, Oceania, South America, and ends in Rio de Janeiro. This girdling of the earth begins in North and ends in South America, so we are looking at an open circle, or really a spiral. The worldwide distribution of this book will spin this still further round the earth.

The other 36 chapters are devoted to various themes that are crucial to this epoch of great transformation in which we humans, and all the other beings of the earthly ecosphere, are presently involved. These themes are discussed in ways that facilitate the transformation of rigid patterns and outdated ideas. To give due place to the holistic principle, the content of every one of the 59 chapters is drawn as well as written. These 59 drawings stand for the right-hand half of our brain and for emo-tional-intuitive thinking. In contrast, the 59 texts correspond to the left half of the brain and logical, rational thinking. If we open the book at any one of the 59 chapters, we will find our thinking and feeling's holistic organization mirrored back to us. In this way we can ensure that what we read does not only add to our store of memory but can actively cooperate in the process of transforming humanity and earth.

To open up yet another way of actively collaborating in building a new community composed of Earth, Humanity and Cosmos, the book proposes exercises related to the themes of individual chapters, which the reader can use to get their own experience of a particular theme. If they wish to enter deeper into the processes of personal and planetary transformation, they can decide to carry out particular exercises regularly over a specific time-period, though being always ready to choose anew...

The book is conceived as a permanent 'stand-by' to counsel and support us through the approaching years of turmoil and pro-found change, and thus improve the odds of our working cre-atively with the process. Every unit is therefore composed so as to be independent. One can open the book at any page and read on from there, or pause at any chapter the instant that one encounters something important.

There is one thing more. The concept of the present book appears very complex and elaborate, and this might be true if we were dealing with a head-type project. But the truth is the very opposite! I was shown in a dream how it is possible to create a book that enables the total and aware Consciousness of Earth to enter into conversation with human beings, and perhaps even further, into practical collaboration.

Let us make the attempt! As you read, please be open to your own inner inspirations. Work with the exercises. Rather than relying on the statements in book, hearken to whatever whispers and stirs in your innermost being.

Marko Pogačnik
Sempas, March 12th, 2006

This work is dedicated to the safe surmounting of the immense difficulties that face Earth and humanity from the threat of global warming and related ecological disasters — those already experienced and those to come.

Earth as a mandala, joining the inner universe to the outer.

1. Earth Space: The Ecosphere of the Earth and Earth Cosmos

Earth is not just an inanimate ball racing through the universe. Above all else, the earth is a point of peace. As the focal point of a multitude of evolutionary strands and living kingdoms, she stands quietly in her place within the cosmos to fulfil her divinely ordered task.

To understand this aright, we should look back to how ancient peoples imagined Earth, and place our planet in the centre of the sacred All. Sun, moon and stars dance around the Earth. In the symbolic language of the old cultures, this means that the earth is primarily a Being who stands in the centre of the cosmos and is open to simultaneous influences received from the whole breadth of the universe, which advance the evolution of life on earth's surface.

Placing the earth in the centre of the universe means that Earth is her own 'I' and is in no way a tributary of the sun, or of any other Being controlled from without. Earth is anchored in her own cosmic centre. The blessings of the life force and wisdom that guide her development find their source in Earth's centre and not in some exterior location in the endless, chaos-attractive galactic space.

Because the mass of humankind has fallen wholesale into the belief that earth is merely a ball circling restlessly round a material sun from which it draws its abundant life, she has been desacralised, secularised and surrendered to boundless exploitation.

Earth carries her own sun in her centre. She is a star that has learned to keep her light focused within and not hurl it wildly to the outside, as does our sun. In this sense, earth is a much older and much wiser star. What Earth projects to the outside is a paradisiacal garden that has gradually evolved on her surface. The light of planet earth streams into the universe in the form of ambrosial flowers, snow covered mountains, silver oceans... To make sure we prevent the destruction of earth's biosphere, our foremost need is to recognize and revere our sister earth in her true identity.

We need to distance ourselves from the intellectual concept of 'earth at the galactic edge,' and instead respect the planet's centring at the galactic midpoint. This means we recognize that Earth is self-aware and thereby also able consciously to fashion the biosphere on her surface, and moreover communicate with us humans and with other beings. If we recognise that Earth, Gaia, is self-aware, a new understanding of the multifarious life on her surface can grow and blossom.

To better enable the multifaceted life on her surface to unfold, Gaia has developed a multidimensional biosphere, the earth space, in which all the beings and evolutionary strands on earth can find the best conditions for their development and extension. Earth space is Earth's maternal body, where all of us have at our disposal a suitable place to live healthily, meaningfully and happily.

However, the concept of earth space is not identical with the biosphere, which refers to the fortunate availability of the physical circumstances permitting life. Earth space means intelligent life joined to the eternity of Being that can only exist when vital-energetic (etheric) forces are also abundantly present and when all levels and beings of the Earth Cosmos are pervaded with the invisible quality of consciousness. Connection to the original space of eternity is also indispensable – we are speaking here of the spiritual dimensions of landscape and earth as a whole.

If the ecosphere of earth is conceived as also containing invisible dimensions – the vital-energetic forces, the all-embracing consciousness and the spiritual plane – then we can speak of the cosmic dimensions of the earth. The earth is no less cosmic than the cosmos itself, of which it is part. The concept of the 'Earth Cosmos' is a healthy alternative to the materialist presentation of a desacralised earth. In the Earth Cosmos, the cosmic and earthly extensions of existence have grown together to form a unique earth space, the 'ecosphere of earth.'

The Earth Cosmos, the ecosphere of earth, is a home to joy, creation and eternal change. Let us learn to know earth space and explore its dimensions!

2. The Epoch of Transformation Has Rung the Doorbell

Uncertainty was the ruling sign as the end approached of the second millennium after the birth of Christ. The ancient prophecies foresaw the end of the world. Ever since I was a small boy, my grandmother had recited the Sybil's prophecy: 'A thousand and another thousand, then never a thousand more.'

In fact, during the autumn of 1997 unusual fluctuations could be perceived in earth's vital-energetic force field. A number of times it looked as if the earth would somersault and stand on its head. I was deeply disquieted. However, one night I was subjected to an avalanche of very impressive dreams, one after the other, and these convinced me that the phenomenon was not a forewarning of global catastrophe. Rather, it was the unleashing of Earth's self-healing process, a sort of global transformation that was of import to earth's ecosphere and all of us earthly beings.

The first of these dreams made me surmise that the subtle planes of the world around us had meanwhile undergone a profound change. The only reason why this passed unnoticed is our obstinate human focus on the material level of existence. In the dream I see myself among a crowd of people who, each absorbed in their own concerns, are walking in all possible directions across a spacious city square. I am racing madly about while I shout with all my strength: 'We think that Reality is still as it always was! That is not true at all! What we see now is only a remembrance of it!'

A second dream made me aware that the calamities that are now happening around us with ever increasing frequency are actually a reflection of the transformative process, which itself is highly positive. It is only because we have no place in our perceptions and consciousness for these swiftly unfolding earth changes that we see them as a series of unfortunate catastrophes. In this dream I find myself climbing down into the cellar of my house when I notice that a wastewater pipe must have broken, for wastewater is shooting out of the stonework. Faced with the likely expense of breaking open the wall to find the damaged pipe, I am in despair. Then, in the very next moment, I become aware that it is not wastewater but crystal-clear spring water that is surging out of the wall into my house cellar.

In fact, at the beginning of 1998 I could confirm that an essential change had occurred in the force fields of the earth. Up to that time the earth element had been the predominant component of the ground radiation. This meant that Earth's consciousness was primarily concentrated on the material plane of existence. In May of that same year this dominant role was taken over by the air element. This signalled that the newly emerging earth space was no longer to be ruled by the dense quality of matter (earth element), but by the much more porous quality of consciousness (air element).

It is hard to describe all that happened in the course of the waves of earth change that followed. The habitual relationship between the earthly and cosmic forces was reversed time and again. The role of animals and elemental beings within the Earth Cosmos was transformed. Outmoded thought patterns and emotional traumas – of humankind as well as localities and countries – thrust themselves out into the light of consciousness to be cleansed and redeemed. Reversals occurred continually and the usual coordinates of earth space were turned on their head.

This change in earth space can be compared with a snake sloughing off its skin. The old skin had become too constricted for earth's further development and in many places begun to burst. That was no cause for alarm! Below the old worn-out skin, a new skin (structured space) had already been prepared, roomier than the old. It will enable the snake – the Earth Cosmos – to develop further.

When the new skin or we may say, the new space, is sufficiently formed, Earth is made free to cast off her old serpent shirt (the old space structure) and enjoy the spaciousness of the new stage in her evolution. In practice, this means that despite the intense inward change, life on the earth's surface still continues to run along its former lines and outwardly shows no essential alteration. It is the invisible, vital-energetic (etheric), emotional and spiritual planes of space that are changed. These are the planes on which the new life and evolutionary space are emerging. When these are sufficiently formed and strong, the old space structure, which we currently inhabit, begins to burst, and it collapses to make space for the new Earth Cosmos.

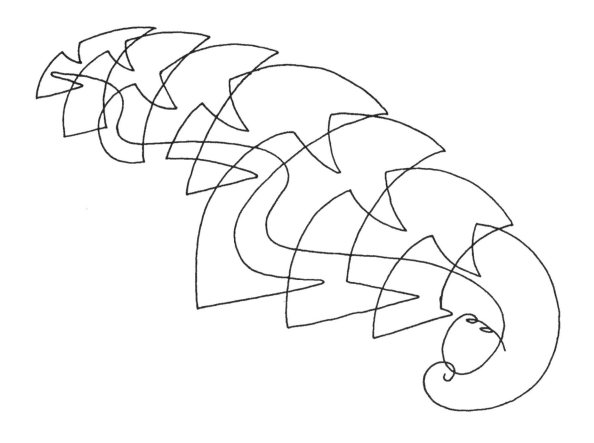

The sloughing of a snake's skin resembles the emergence of new space.

The interdimensional doorway in Central Park, Manhattan

3. New York: The Megaliths of Manhattan

Mention the 'megaliths of Manhattan' and one immediately thinks of the giant skyscrapers of New York, reminiscent of disproportionately huge standing stones. However, strangely enough, in the middle of Manhattan's cityscape one can actually find mighty blocks of granite whose function is related to the megaliths of Neolithic Europe.

Of course, you will not find them standing in the right-angled criss-cross of Manhattan's avenues and streets. There, every last square meter is put to practical use. They stand in the middle of Manhattan Island, in the part that was left free when the rest was urbanized. Here you will find, on a giant scale, a nearly natural park landscape called 'Central Park'.

Apart from the fountains, sports grounds and other installations that properly belong to a distinguished city park, the original rock landscape of Manhattan has been well preserved within Central Park. We are looking at an undulating skin of black granite, mostly covered by earth and plant growth. It is only here and there that the black granite juts from the ground in the shape of a hill of rock, rubbed smooth during the last Ice Age by the Wisconsin Glacier.

Given the smoothness of their surface, it is the glacier that appears responsible for all the black granite blocks that its icy tongue is thought to have transported here from the far north. They lie along Central Park's long axis, apparently randomly distributed. However, precise observation leads to the conclusion that the granite blocks have been carefully set in place. Some are positioned on the rounded granite heads of the parent rock, others are raised aloft by smaller, underlying rocks, as was done to construct prehistoric dolmens.

Could it be that they once stood along Manhattan's entire axis, that is, along the present Sixth Avenue (Avenue of the Americas) in the south and St. Nicholas Avenue in the north? Anyway, it is only in the southern expanse of Central Park, where the land has been left to nature, that the significant granite rocks are still preserved. One can clearly sense that the megaliths of Central Park were put in place according to a definite plan. If one invokes

their message, what one finds most remarkable is the unusual strength of their radiation.

Perception indicates that there are two quite different phases to their presence. On one plane they present themselves as unusual rocks, even radiating in geometrical patterns, while on a second plane they change into beings that are immemorially old and wise. One then senses them to be affectionate friends of cosmic origin. One could say that they are cosmic elemental beings.

What could be the role of these rocks that are beings? They stand or lie along Manhattan's long axis, which is actually a rift in the earth: not a geological one certainly, but an etheric rift that leads deep into the nether world. The world below Manhattan resembles a giant storehouse of the forces of life, and through this storehouse of elemental power runs the etheric rift; though this is not so much an etheric rift as an energetic doorway. This doorway to Manhattan's nether world bears an imprint like a furrow in earth's original sea.

The probable role of the Manhattan megaliths was to open or close this doorway as needed. There was a long pause while they 'slept', and the doorway remained closed. However, since the catastrophe of September 11, 2001, when the twin towers of the World Trade Centre were destroyed, they have awakened[1].

This doorway guarded by the megaliths of Manhattan enables earth's outer and inner universes to communicate; and at this time of earth transformation this kind of communication takes on decisive importance. This is why the megaliths in New York were rudely awoken by the catastrophic blow to the Twin Towers. However, the subsequent and newly manifest opening of the interdimensional doorway in Manhattan accords only in part with the positioning of the megaliths. In the last few years the doorway has taken a zigzag line that runs the length of Central Park and also includes some of the old megaliths.

The corridor that leads between the wide expanses of the Cosmos and the interior of earth, to which New York, seat of earth's United Nations, imparts its planetary significance, is once more open!

---

[1] As new populations replaced the original builders, the stones' function was forgotten and they fell into disuse. Ignored by the local tribes, they 'slept'. They were awoken by the shocking impact of 9/11 on the present human population.

Exercise 2, for grounding your head (the Manhattan-exercise)

1. Bend forwards till you are nearly touching the earth with your out-stretched hands. Imagine that your hands are reaching right down into the earth's centre.

2. Now stand up slowly and as you do so, draw your connection with the earth's centre upwards along your own axis. In the process, lay the palms of your hands one upon the other.

3. When you reach the level of your heart, point your fingertips upwards.

4. Lift your hands up higher. As soon as they reach the level of your face, you should pause for a moment in front of the third eye with your hands together as in prayer.

5. After a while, stretch your arms out to left and right as far as they will go. As you do so, watch how your headspace is opening.

6. Now bend once more towards the ground and do the exercise again as before. Then repeat it a few more times.

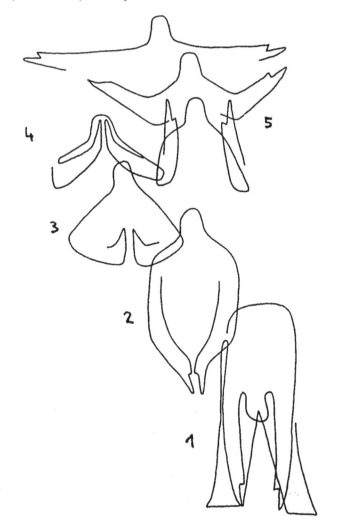

Exercise 1, for the experience of earth space

After you have settled yourself for meditation, imagine that you are sitting in the exact centre of the earth.

Forget all the tales you've heard about the heat in the earth's centre, purgatory and so on; instead, be open to whatever experience wants to surface.

Your centre, which is usually situated in the region of your navel, is identical with the centre of the earth.

The life forms of earth are developing constantly on all sides of you. Trees are growing above and below, to left and to right. Birds too are flying about on all sides...Let your imagination be creative!

Now let the images go. Forget them and look instead at what your feelings tell you, and what the experience is bringing you.

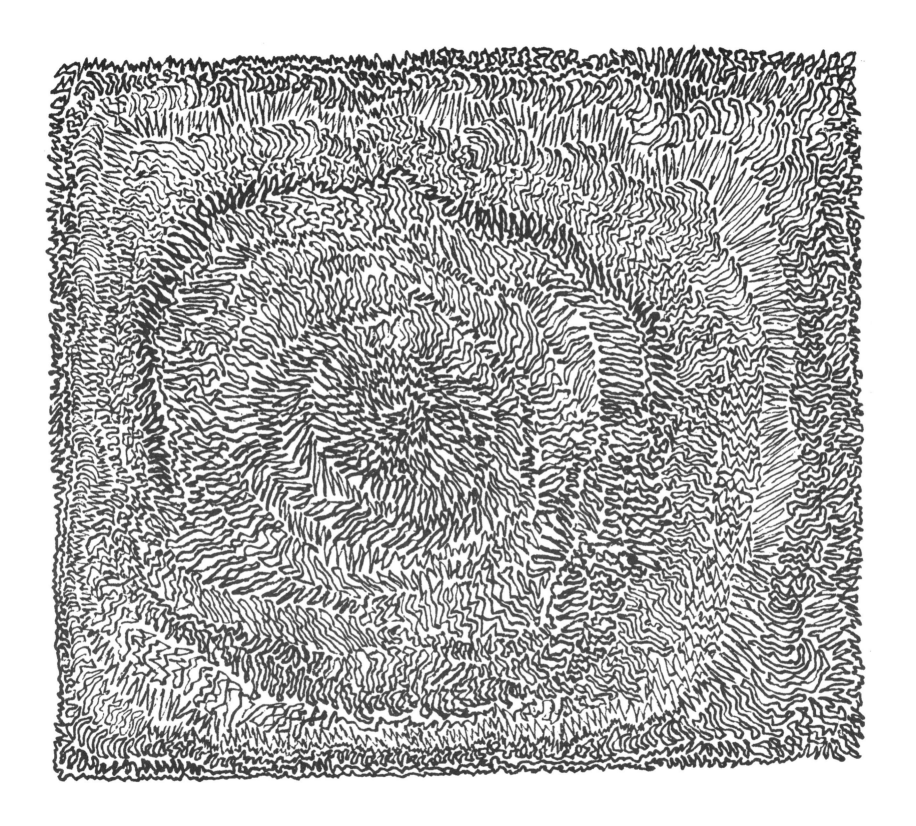

Energetic Drawing 1

The inner and the outer universes intersect fork-shaped, with the disc of the earth in the centre.

4. A Synergetic Image of the World

Nobody thought that the earth could be a lifeless ball before the intellect's view of the universe had gained the upper hand. In fact, this rounded earth is a mirror image of the human intellect, which recognises only the outward phenomena of creation and is uninterested in her inner roots. If you are really standing on a ball, your attention has to be directed to the outside. By imagining earth to be a mere ball, humankind has been pressured into the desolate vistas of the purely external. The eyes of powerful telescopes flit incessantly across the nightly heavens, but nowhere do they find a human-related soul. In the midst of a universe abrim with life, we are like to perish of loneliness.

Quite otherwise was the world vision held by the first cultures, based on their experience of the Earth Being. In the famous Slovenian legend of the fish woman Faronika, the earth is represented as a disc borne on the back of the archetypal fish. The health or otherwise of life on the surface is dependent on what happens in the earth's interior. The fish woman Faronika puts it this way: 'If I flick my tail, the world will perish! If I turn on my back, the world will flood!'

One can view the fish woman Faronika as a pictorial representation of the Earth Soul, meaning the planet's inner 'I' that guides life's processes and the transformations on the earth's surface. The luck, or alternatively the misfortune, of beings on the surface is dependent on the harmony that exists between the intentions of the soul and the rhythms of the earth body. This is the reason why primeval cultures have so carefully nurtured their relationship with 'Mother Earth', erecting stone circles, positioning menhirs, celebrating rituals...

In this epoch of profound transformation, it is undesirable for people to hold onto the idea of earth as a soulless ball, closed in upon itself. However, neither is it desirable to return to the old vision of earth as a circular disc. Can both pictures of the world be tied together in a synergistic knot? Such a possibility must exist, given the diversity of dimensions contained in the universe.

Let us take as our model a fork-shaped picture of the world. To one side of the fork the expanses of the All spread out through the outwardly visible reaches of interstellar space. On the other side they are ranged inward, in the direction of earth's centre. There lies a multi-layered netherworld that withdraws itself from our gaze. The fork-shaped universe spreads both outward and inward. Just as the expansive dimensions of heaven are inhabited by different beings and civilizations, so also are the layers of space in earth's interior, though these appear to be becoming ever tighter and narrower.

However, it is only in appearance that the space in earth's interior seems narrower as one draws closer to its centre. The reverse is true if viewed from the dimensions of soul and spirit, which belong to the limitless space of eternity: then earth's interior space becomes ever broader. This context offers a new interpretation of the image of the earth as a circular disc. In this, each separate landscape of the earth's surface is perceived as a disc-shaped entity or Holon. Each entity (Holon) of the earth acts as a sensitive membrane that lies at the point of intersection between the outer aspects of the universe and the expansive inner aspect. Thus every Holon is individual and brings a particular quality to the wholeness of the earth.

Every single Holon of the earth lies at the point of intersection between 'heaven' and the 'netherworld'. The outward and the inward related expanses of our universe communicate with each other through each and every one of earth's disc-shaped membranes to support and further the wonderful life on the surface. Earth's particular miracle which enables Spirit to embody in matter can only happen if forces and bits of information can flow through the earth membrane from the interior universe into the outer, and vice-versa.

How can this multidimensional worldview be harmonised with the rounded form of planet earth? By recognising that earth's individual holographic entities (the disc-shaped membranes) complement each other to finally form the mega-membrane, which we know as the round ball of earth.

5. The Worlds of Inward Earth

The spiritual view of life has had the tragic side-effect of turning humanity away from the real Being of Earth. Instead of directing our steps towards the wellspring of life, to earth's centre, it has guided our attention to the 'frigidity' of the physical universe. Together, let us summon the courage to resist the intellect's conviction and its apparent power until such time as the voice of the heart, our intuition, has secured equivalent status within our sphere of consciousness.

Astrology is a useful aid in this endeavour: it helps us recognise the deeper significance of the outward universe and so decipher the message conveyed by the separate planets and the whole circle of the zodiac. Over the last two decades geomancy has been rebuilt and offers a path to help humanity reconnect with the multidimensional earth. The practice focuses on the centres of the landscape, the vital-energetic force fields and the extensions of their consciousness. Furthermore, geomancy introduces us to the archetypical strata of earth consciousness, composed of the inward universe in the centre of the earth and the worlds and civilizations that inhabit the earth's interior.

Here we strike against a reef of weighty prejudices and traumas that obstruct our free enjoyment of the synergetic worldview. Of these, the weightiest is the projection of a hell existing in the earth's interior. Masking its worries in a religious veil, the mind agonises that the earth's centre must be a dreadful place where we pay for the sins we have committed on its surface. The worlds of the earth's centre, and with them all the soul-oriented extensions of the earth, are thereby subjected to the severest taboo. Scientific thinking has replaced this horrific picture with one no less dreadful: that of a superheated core at the earth's centre. People may feel they have no alternative but to turn away from the repugnant world of inward earth and put their exclusive faith in what is external to it.

More can still be said about the projection of a hell: there is an undeniable need for a space where transformation can happen. Part of the process of human evolution is to be confronted with the truth, beyond any possibility of illusion. In practice, this happens in spaces that encourage the discharge of the after-death-processes. Such spaces may be sought among the layers of earth's inward universe. However, as suggested above, the mind has played a trick on us: it has placed the setting of the halls of transformation in the consciousness of all cultures in such fashion that they conceal the Being of Earth. They deny the divine nature of their core, distort the beloved essence of Earth's inner universe and become projections of horror.

On the other hand and more positively, we are frequently being confronted with messages that obviously originate in the sphere of consciousness at the earth's centre: for example, the crop circles that every year appear in fields worldwide. Some unknown force bends the plant stems from within so that they are laid down in precise geometric patterns. The symbolic content of the individual crop circles and their geometrical language are clearly related to the most varied cultures on the earth's surface. Also, one can recognise the expression of earth's consciousness in the familiar earthiness of the cosmic radiation that emanates from the crop circles.

We may suppose that crop circles express an inner-earthly intelligence that shares cultural and civilizing experiences similar to our own on the earth's surface, although it presumably exists on other planes of being than we incarnate humans. There is a suggestion of parallel civilizations occupying different layers of earth's inward universe. They are trying to communicate in a language that is known to us from our own experience.

We may rejoice that it is not the fate of crop circles — stunning messages from earth's centre — to be burdened with projections of hell, but they are nonetheless threatened. False imitations hide the original quality of their message and sow doubt as to their credibility. Obviously, people will shy away from any ready acceptance of a voice from the earth's interior. To put it more precisely, we shy away from the destruction of the old, one-sided worldview that 'protects' us from the wisdom and love of the Earth Being.

External worlds and the worlds of inward earth.

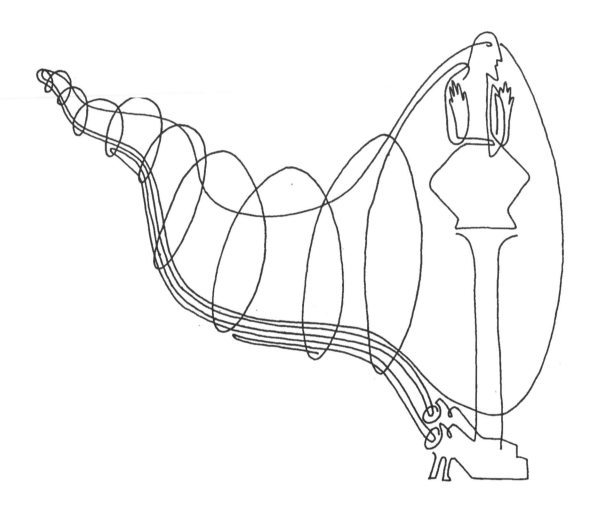

The central column of the 'Portico de la Gloria' as the conclusion of the pilgrim way to Santiago.

6. Santiago de Compostella, Spain: The Path of the Heart

Legend tells us that the waves of the Atlantic Ocean cast the coffin bearing the mortal remains of Saint James onto the west coast of Spain. This was James the Elder, brother of Jesus Christ, who earlier had died a martyr's death in Jerusalem. After James' coffin emerged in miraculous fashion at Santiago de Compostella, the most important pilgrim route of western culture began to take shape. The first pilgrim to take the 'Path of the Heart' is thought to have been Charlemagne at the end of the eighth century. In the following centuries the network of roads that led to Santiago spread throughout Europe, from as far away as Finland, Poland and Sicily. Today, every year, countless thousands of pilgrims still make their way to Santiago.

This designation of the pilgrim road to Santiago as the 'Path of the Heart', what does it mean? If we speak of the power of the heart, we are thinking of a power that is capable of bringing even unconquerable opposites into creative relationship with each other. It is from the field of tension that thrums between the cosmic opposites that is born the quality that we call love.

After travelling hundreds of kilometres, pilgrims always perform a ritual at the Cathedral of Santiago. It takes place in front of the Romanesque 'Portico de la Gloria,' the cathedral's main doorway. The pilgrims walk slowly in a long file round the doorway's central column. The top of the column bears a magnificent representation of Jesus Christ and illustrates the expanses of the celestial universe. At the bottom, and therefore on the ground, are two leonine-style dragons, chiselled with wide-open jaws. The pilgrims first touch the area at the top of the column, to affirm their relationship with the heavens. Afterwards, they walk round the column and stick both hands into the dragons mouths, symbolically touching the depths of the inward universe and participating in the vibration of the nether world.

After a pilgrim has touched the two opposite extensions of the universe, the invisible part of the ritual begins to unfold. This is its spiritual superstructure, on which the majority of pilgrims regrettably miss out. They are exclusively interested in the ritual's formal side, and usually take particular care to be photographed as they perform it. The Christ figure at the upper end of the column shows what occurs during the ritual's spiritual superstructure. The figure's hands, held at heart level, are opened like the two wings of a gate, meaning that the gates in front of the heart chakra are open. Thus the human being begins to shine, radiating the power of love.

The closing ritual in the cathedral of Santiago is constructed on the same model as the pilgrim way itself. The pilgrim road from Pamplona across Leon to Santiago resembles a tunnel of light through which the pilgrims move. One can compare this light tunnel with the central column of the cathedral door. Above the light tunnel runs a soul pathway. In geomancy the concept of the soul pathway signifies a power highway along which move those souls of humankind that at the time are not embodied in matter. They inhabit the celestial universe and glide along such soul pathways to pursue their goals in the hereafter.

The soul pathway represents the outwardly oriented viewpoint of the universe that we have labelled 'heaven.' On the pilgrim road to Santiago in contrast, the inward space of earth is represented by the strong currents of archetypal earthly power that underlie the pilgrim route. They represent a kind of foundation on which the light tunnel was gradually built. Over the centuries, the persistent movement of pious pilgrims along the route has provided sufficient light-forces for its construction.

Taking the viewpoint of the individual human being, the soul pathway above the tunnel corresponds to a tiny chakra situated above the neck chakra. Also, the stream of elemental power below the light tunnel corresponds to an equally small chakra lying below the sex chakra. When human beings make their way along the pilgrim road to Santiago, these two chakras are activated by their resonance with both 'storeys' of the tunnel. In consequence, the heart chakra that vibrates in the middle between them awakens and begins to shine.

Exercise 3, to experience the inward space of earth

In an upright, easy but formal attitude you slowly stride over the earth's surface.

As you do so, you perceive that the earth's surface resembles a thick film of matter.

You are simultaneously striding on the underside of this film, with your head pointing downwards.

Continue further and keep this image in your imagination.

Allow both your bodies, the one above and the one below, to gradually glide into one another.

What are the feelings that arise in you? What experiences penetrate you?

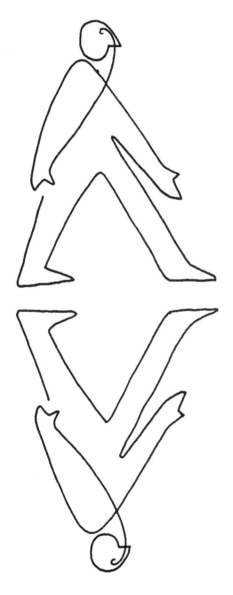

Exercise 4, to strengthen the relationship with the earth's centre

Seat yourself and be present in your heart centre.

Imagine that you are building a light bridge that projects out from your heart centre, then jumps up over your head and runs away towards your backspace.

Now imagine yourself tiny, and run over this bridge towards the space that is hiding behind your back.

There, at the level of your sex chakra, you find a deep, round well.

You climb down the well shaft and reach the surface of the water.

Dive down into the water till you arrive at the well bottom.

Actually, there is no bottom, but instead a bright opening.

After going through the opening, you find yourself in the space of earth's inward universe.

Absorb the experience of this space. Take it into your heart centre. Then return by the same path as that by which you entered this experience.

Savour the quality of the experience in your heart.

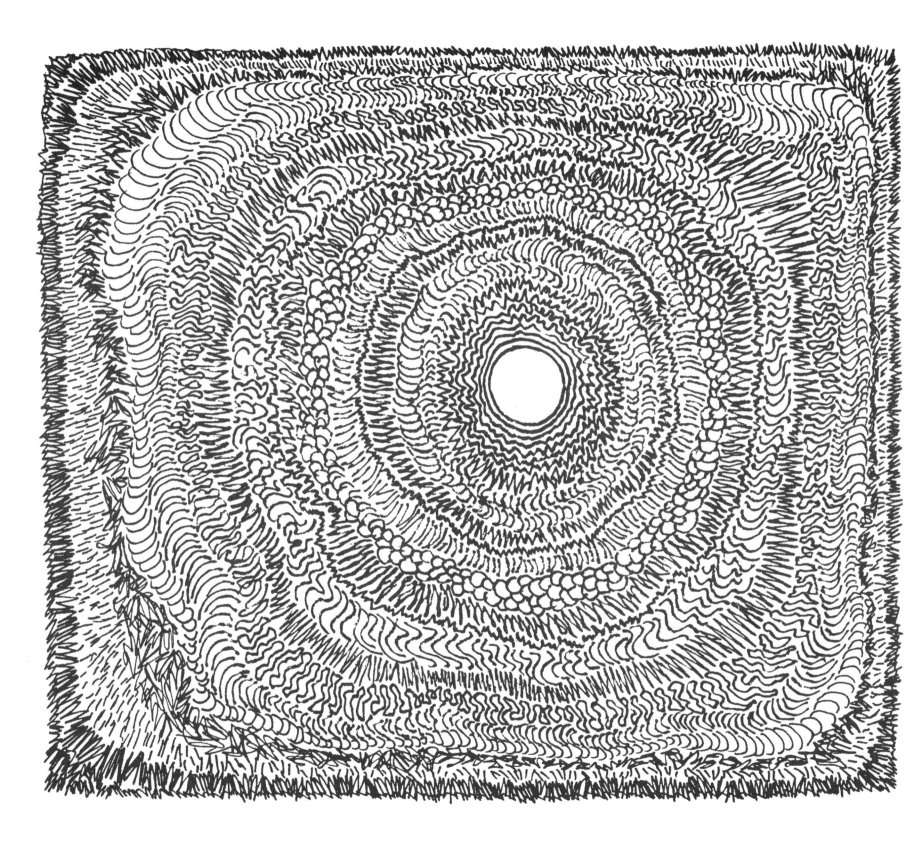

Energetic Drawing 2

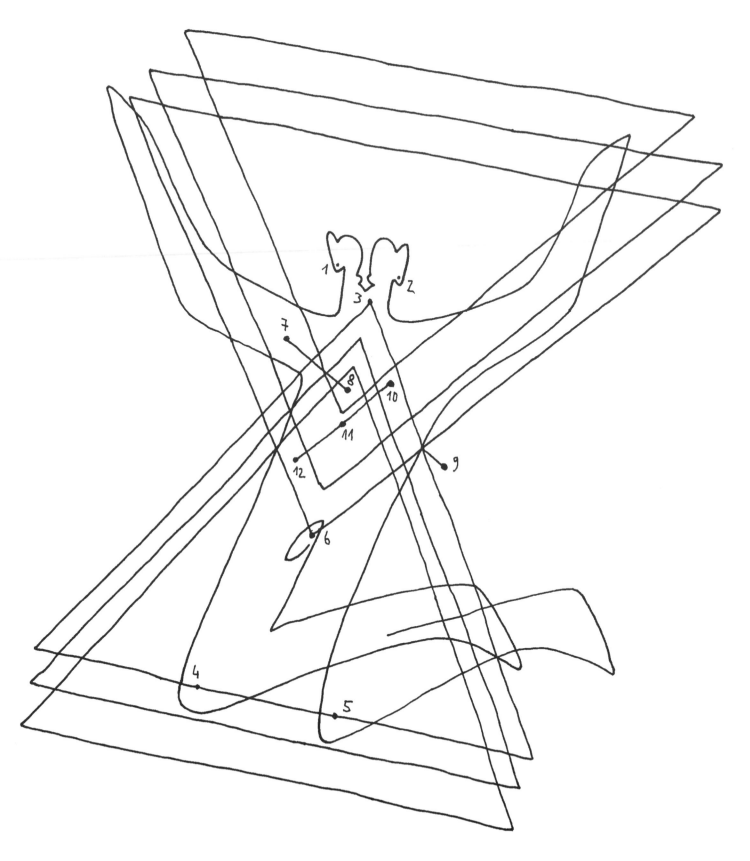

The chakras of the heart systems: the system of the 'third ear' (1-3); the system of the 'third knee' (4-6); the heart channel (7-9); the system of the elemental heart (10-12).

7. Earth and the Human Being as a Heart System

The Star of David, when projected onto the human body, is the best model for comprehending the workings of the heart system. Two triangles compose the Star of David, and the one with its point directed upwards corresponds to the spiritual forces that are concentrated in the area of the head. The triangle with the point directed downwards symbolizes the earthly forces whose focus lies in the area of the sex organs. The heart chakra sits in the exact centre between these two energetic extremes of spirit and matter. They are contrarily charged and your classic role should be to hold these two opposites together, as if they are two wild horses each trying to tear off in its own direction. It is this subtle energetic relationship of spirit and matter that characterises the human being, and it is the heart centre that should prevent it from becoming lost.

The epochal change, which is happening right now and in which we are participating, has brought in its wake a fundamental inversion of this relationship. It is best described by the words of Jesus Christ: 'The first shall be last' and vice-versa. Translated into the language of the body, this statement means that the cosmic forces of heaven are no longer stuck in the area of the head. The impulse of change has caused them to move and they are descending through all the bodily planes to reach the full flower of their presence in the area of the sex organs. It is here that the spiritual forces' drive towards incarnation is focused. Concretely, this works through a little known chakra that belongs to the heart system and is situated below our sex organs. One could call it the 'chakra of the third knee,' because it is located in a triangle that it forms with the two earth element chakras that pulsate behind the knee.

In contrast, the earthly forces of our heart system, originating in the inward earth, rise upwards through all the planes of the body towards the head. Their ascent is focused on a point above the neck chakra. We can call this focus point the 'chakra of the third ear,' for it stands in a triangular relationship with the two chakras located on the earlobes. The highest now finds its expression at the body's lowest point and, quite reversed, the lowest expresses itself through the heart system's uppermost chakra. This perfect interlacing of the heavenly and earthly within us makes possible the birth of a wonderful child in the centre of our being. This child embodies a loving power that teaches us to develop compassion for all other living beings, visible and invisible. It is this power of love that inspires humankind to participate in a spectrum involving the most different kinds of loving relationships, whereby we contribute to the universal evolutionary process and also get to shout aloud for joy.

From an energetic point of view, the human being is really little more than a gigantic and unbelievably potent heart system that pulsates between the knee chakras and the earlobes. The heart chakra rests in the midst between them and derives its power from the functioning of the 'heart channel.' This runs from the chakra of the cosmic heart at the back to the efflux chakra located in front of the breast. The role of the heart channel is to ensure that the constant outflow of our heart force at the front is balanced by quiet participation in the effusion of the Godhead's love entering through the chakra in the back.

To these must be added the system of the 'elemental heart.' This system is a holographic fragment of earth's heart that beats in the human as a nature being. The three chakras of this system are located along the diagonal that joins the heart muscle chakra with a chakra designated by the fifth stigmata of Christ.

Just like the human being, the entire surface of earth is also pervaded by a heart system. The planetary heart system is focused around Tibet. Also, each landscape and every place within it has its own heart centre. Their resonance binds them together to form a contiguous system. The task of a heart centre is to ensure the free flow and constant regeneration of the forces of life on the earth's surface. Their action stimulates the original paradisiacal quality of earthly life. One could compare the action of the heart centres to the love of the Earth Mother, which is given to all beings on her surface – and to us humans too, if we are open to it.

8. The Space of Love!

Tradition has handed down the idea of a 'golden age', meaning an epoch when the earth's ecosphere was constructed quite differently from what we see today. 'Milk and honey' could flow freely because human awareness was still open to the impulses of the Earth Soul. The unhindered pulsation of the paradisiacal quality of Earth's consciousness in the here and now, and the free flow of its forces, brought into being a spatial structure that gave humanity the blessed feeling of being invited into the wholeness of the universe.

The deeper the slide into the age of bronze, the more that spatial quality was influenced by the mental projections of the then current bellicose culture. Humanity certainly built new mythical images of the Wholeness, but its all-round (and real) presence within the earthly cosmos was lost. The spatial structure grew still more inflexible when its arrangement followed the intellect's logically conditioned projections. Nowadays and in every instant, billions of people confirm the spatial structure as being exclusively material and put it to work as such. In consequence we must endure living in a space that broadly excludes the fullness and diversity of life. This straitjacket causes the various peoples each to strengthen their own particular space, which leads to war and allows fellow humans to starve…

Is there no alternative path that could create a more loving space? Perhaps, on condition that the human being learns to embody the principles of universal love. The force of love is in no way a purely sweet force. The force of love is primarily a force for change. Whoever loves cannot remain who they were. And whoever is beloved begins to dismantle their egocentric fortress and is challenged to reveal their inner truth.

If we become capable of creating a space for a civilization that is based on loving relationships and is constructed from the heart systems of earth and humanity, then part of the bargain is that we first undergo a shattering transformation. Why is this? It is because the old space holds firmly to particular coordinates that are based on the past spiritual achievements of certain human beings who put their stamp on western and eastern cultures. Contrarily, the new space is dependent on the quality of the relationships that vibrate between humans in the given moment, and respectively, between humans and the beings of earth and heaven.

It is no longer possible to find support in values that were enthroned in the past. In this newly forming, erotically conditioned life space, all that counts is what is true in the moment and illuminated from within by the heart's unhindered light. All else is as ground-up dust. At first, the human being feels lost in a chaos that lacks clear definitions. We ask, how can a universe possibly exist whose characteristic is to hinder the building of firmly based structures before they are even started? It appears there is nothing within this chaos to help persons connect and find their orientation. However, there still remains the possibility of loving and developing compassion for the other beings of the visible and invisible cosmos of life. It is possible to BE.

Another kind of social order arises from the liberated love impulse: an order that forbids the persistent wearing of masks, so denying to others the individual light of one's presence; an order that forbids the oppression of fellow humans and other beings in their appointed roles, which they must fulfil to maintain our given world-image from collapse. When Eros becomes the foundation of earth's ecosphere, we will participate in an open, multidimensional space. The mental structures that define earth's space at the present time are then replaced by erotic relationships that are included in all dimensions and woven into and nourished by the participants on all planes. The basis is free choice. The prerequisite is not to let the heart's unsuspected power frighten us away. The issue is to discover the erotic architecture of life's space. However, one can undertake absolutely nothing in this direction if one has neglected to open one's own heart and practice the intuition of the heart.

The Goddess of Love; love that transforms, blesses and protects.

The composition of 'Grail Landscape Temples' throughout the world,
extended on either side between the angelic world and the Earth Soul.

9. Rennes le Chateau: Landscape Temple of the Grail

Tradition tells us that after Christ's crucifixion, Mary Magdalene took the grail to Europe and brought it to Rennes le Chateau in southern France. The grail is the chalice from which Jesus Christ drank at the Last Supper before his crucifixion, and which he lifted on high to bless his succession on earth. Of course, by Christ's succession is meant not only priests and devotees but all people who are ready to pass through a particular transformation. This is a fundamental transformation in the course of which the average human being, limited and of little faith, becomes a microcosm who is able to reflect the divine breadth of the universe. It is Christ who has revealed to us this stunning possibility for our further evolution. However, to render the possibility real, the action must include the feminine forces of the universe, i.e., the forces of the Goddess, because it is the Goddess who teaches how spiritual visions can become manifest and lived in daily life.

Mary Magdalene, depicted in the church at Rennes le Chateau with the chalice in one hand and a skull in the other, represents the forces of God's feminine aspect, i.e., of the Goddess. Apart from the Goddess, there is no known instrument able to create the transformation symbolised by the skull, and thereby actualize the embryo of the new human being in our interior. In alchemical language, lead is transformed into gold. The chalice in the sainted Magdalene's other hand is a successor to the archetypical grail that represents the pregnant belly of Mother Earth and symbolises the transference of spirit into the world of matter. The universal Goddess invented the process by which invisible spirit can embody itself in matter by herself incarnating in terrestrial matter.

Where in the landscape of the Rennes le Chateau plateau do we find the counterpart to the legend of the Grail and the sainted Magdalene? We are drawn to the ambience of the village church (meanwhile become famous). The place is characterised by a divine presence of exceeding density. The church and its surroundings are located within a huge pillar of light, signifying angelic presences. The light pillar indicates that the plateau of

Rennes le Chateau is an extraordinary place that plays a definite role in the landscape temple of Languedoc, which stretches from the Mediterranean Sea to the Pyrenees Mountains. This landscape temple of Languedoc is centred on a hallowed mountain named Montsegur, which derives its holiness from the mighty heart centre that pulsates in the mountain's midst. Like a green sun, the heart centre of Montsegur radiates its beams through the entire area.

The sequel to the legend of the Holy Grail will help us reconstruct the landscape temple in the local countryside. During the merciless crusade against the Cathars, the grail that Mary Magdalene had brought to Rennes le Chateau was hidden in the fortress on the summit of Montsegur. Before the fortress fell, it is thought that the chalice was carried secretly over the cliffs and chasms around Montsegur to be taken deeper into the Pyrenees. And there, in one of the many grottoes around Ussat-les-Bains, the grail cup is still hidden today.

The grail's legendary journey from Rennes le Chateau to Montsegur, and from thence to the grottoes of the Pyrenees, corresponds to the three-part composition of the local landscape temples. The grottoes in the area between Ussat-les-Bains and Montrealp des Sos represent the Earth Soul's relationship to the nether world – or should we say they relate to her focus on the realm of earth's centre. In contrast, the plateau of Rennes le Chateau acts as an antenna for the forces of heaven and the angelic world. The 'grail mountain' of Montsegur lies in the middle between them. The power of Montsegur's heart centre is such as to cause the two extremities to combine and synthesise. In this manner its interior creative power is developed to the point that it is able to get life to express itself through 'dead' matter: this is the power of the Grail. The grail landscape temple in Languedoc is only one of the numerous grail landscapes worldwide. Their probable task is to care for the fertility of the earth's surface and inspire us humans to develop and radiate our true identity.

Exercise 5, to support
the development of the heart system

This exercise is inspired by Jesus Christ's saying about the grain of mustard seed, how the most luxuriant plant grows from the smallest seed.

Feel for your heart centre and see it as a tiny ball of light (like a grain of mustard seed).

Imagine that you are slowly rolling that little ball of light around in your heart centre, as if it were a bead in a rosary. You can help your imagination if you hold one of your hands upright and rub the tips of the other hand's index and middle fingers against the ball of its thumb.

There are similar little balls of light in the spiritual focus below the sex chakra and in the earthly focus above the larynx. You should roll these around too, switching alternately between the two foci.

After a while, forget the balls of light and listen to the quality of your heart system. When your concentration begins to falter, you can return to rolling the balls of light...

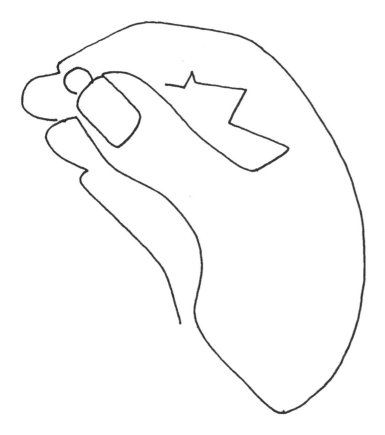

Exercise 6, to experience the quality of the heart force

Seat yourself and be still.

Imagine the landscape around you to be filled with the riches of its life and people...You are encircled by life, as if by a sphere.

From your heart centre, send out your love to every side of the sphere of life.

Now concentrate on your heart centre itself.

Imagine yourself getting nearer and nearer to your heart centre.

As you go deeper and deeper into your heart centre, you simultaneously broaden the scope of your love to send it wider and wider to the outside.

You are travelling ever further within and ever further outside, both at the same time.

After a while your heart space becomes so broad, you can forget the exercise. Just be present in the breadth of your heart.

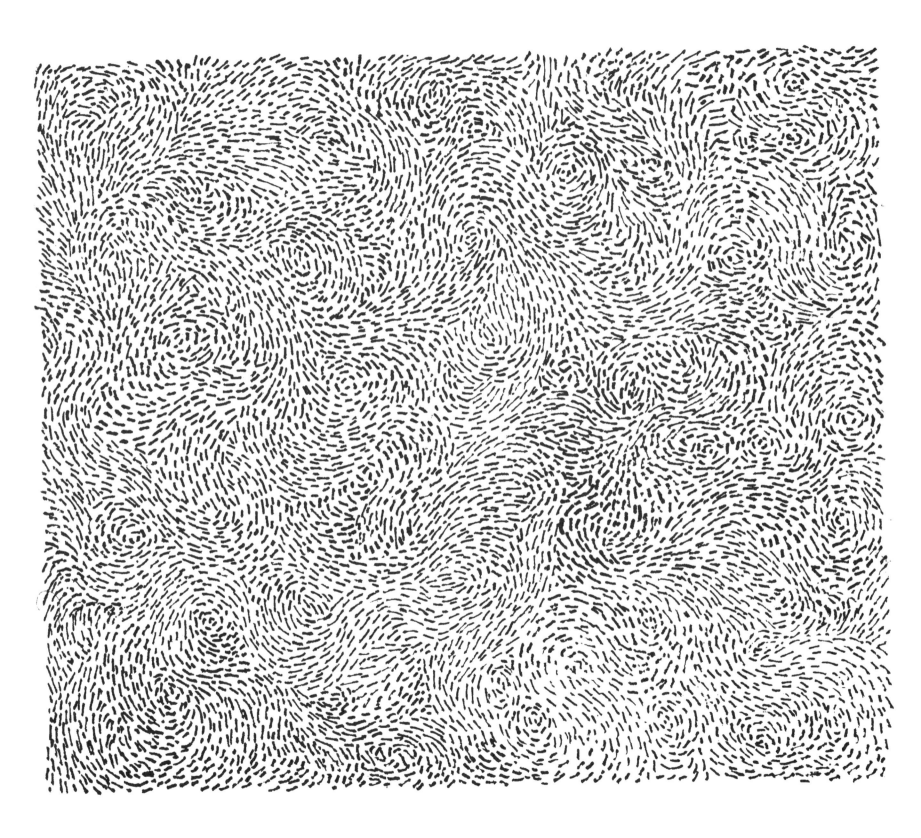

Energetic Drawing 3

The inner child as symbol of the eternal soul that mediates

between the spirit above and the incarnate human below.

10.   Religion of the Soul

When human beings began to wander ever more frequently along paths that alienated them from their inner being, the Masters of Eternity sought feverishly for means to stop humankind getting lost in the labyrinth of time. A kind of compass was developed. It is called 'religion', i.e., belief. Modern humans have certainly lost the immediate feeling of eternity's constant presence in their lives. We no longer have the ability to use prayer to weave each separate moment of our lives into the fabric of eternity. However, with the help of the different religions, we have learned to believe that we partake of eternity by being human, and that death has no final validity. Enlightened women and men have incarnated in earth's most different cultures and provided humanity with various tools of faith. The divine underpinnings given to the foundations of individual religions should guarantee to hold a person harmless for any sort of belief untested by their own experience. Thus it is explicitly stated that the Koran was written according to the pronouncements of the Archangel Gabriel, and that Christianity was founded by Jesus of Nazareth who was an Anointed One (i.e., a Christ). The religious institutions built upon these roots have the task of watching over the credibility of the corresponding religious traditions.

The plan to rescue us estranged humans has been further developed from millennium to millennium, but during the last two centuries we have been witnesses to a dangerous upset, for many people, simultaneously, have begun to distance themselves from the traditional forms of belief.

Are we in danger of becoming a sacrifice, the same danger from which the Masters of Eternity wished to save us when they invented the numerous religions? Or are we a race renewed, capable of immediate union with the root of Being and of vibrating consciously with our own divine self?

It is no accident that humanity's adverse attitude towards religious practices surfaced towards the end of the 18th Century, i.e., at exactly the same time as we were recognising the value of personal freedom. That meant that we could now freely choose whether to continue with our belief in the reality of eternity, or whether we would prefer to take steps towards attaining the immediate experiences that accompany the personal participation in the vibrations of divinity. We have become free to tread our personal spiritual path.

This may be an outcome devoutly to be wished, but there is no denying the danger that a person may become a sacrifice to the egocentric, quasi-spiritual type of attitude and thenceforth wander around in an illusory world. To avoid this danger, one must develop one's communication with one's own soul, one's inner 'I'. It is really true that the essence of the human being vibrates (through the Higher Self) as a holographic fragment of the Godhead. On the other hand, a person is still incarnate in the temporal and spatial limits of the terrestrial world, and therefore feels separated from the eternal nature of the divine self. We can overcome this fateful separation if we invite the middle limb of our tripartite nature – our eternal soul – into the re-unification process. Our soul, which is an individuation of the all-embracing Higher Self, knows the meaning and direction of our personal development. It has guided our steps from one incarnation to another, and stored up our experiences on the way. The soul knows which are the true life tasks we have undertaken, and how we can evade habitual aberrations and illnesses.

If human beings are prepared to listen to the voice of their own soul, they will need no other mediator to build the bridge between body and spirit. The soul speaks through the language of the heart, through feelings that vibrate deep in the lower body. It expresses itself in dreams and daily events that the soul itself sets in motion, so that the resulting experiences may provide the person with some particular gift. There is no doubt, however, that the human being needs shamans, priests and religious environments to be intermediaries until we have learned to listen to the voice of our own soul, and to follow her directions.

11.   This Earth's League of Beings

The multitudinous diversity of plants and animals that live upon the earth is quite incredible! One could spend a whole lifetime, just learning to know them and admire their peculiarities. The wealth of earthly life becomes even more amazing when one begins to perceive the invisible dimensions of the earthly ecosphere. Then one realizes how many fields of life have been excluded from our consciousness due to our intellect's limited ability to interpret complex perceptions. Among these we can count the evolution of the elemental beings. We are speaking of the missing link between the sphere of earth consciousness in the inward earth, and the materialised form of the plants, minerals, animals *and humans* on the earth's surface.

The evolution of the countless life forms on the earth's surface can be viewed as a multidimensional creative process. The creative action begins right in the earth's centre, in the sphere of earth consciousness (i.e., the Earth Soul), or put poetically, in the sphere of Gaia. There the thoughts are born that to a large extent fashion and steer the life on the earth's surface. But how could Gaia's messages and instructions reach the plants, animals and other beings of the ecosphere if there were no elemental beings to serve as messengers? Yet elemental beings are more than mere bearers of directive impulses from the heart of the Earth Soul. Their particularity of lacking a physical body enables them to slip into the subtle bodily structures of plants, humans, etc., and from moment to moment transfer the instructions of the earth consciousness.

Insofar as the intellect of modern humans can admit the possible existence of elemental beings, we must forthwith free ourselves from the traditional representations of fairies and dwarves. Elemental beings are not form-conditioned entities. Rather they should be viewed as a kind of consciousness-cell that has a body assembled from life forces and specific qualities of feeling. They are born from the consciousness of Earth's Soul, and are there dissolved again when they have completed their task on the earth's surface. Consequently, there are elemental beings that bring in specific impulses and whose existence is only momentary. However, there are also the mighty bearers of the consciousness of landscapes and mountain chains, the so-called 'devas' whose service lasts through millennia.

The angels are another evolutionary thread that belongs to our earth's league of beings. Thus, just as one can say of elemental beings that they incorporate earth consciousness, one can represent angels as 'incorporating' the consciousness of the universe. Different qualities of divine consciousness and presence that are widespread and supportive within the universe are incorporated in different kinds (hierarchies) of angel. Angels, although cosmic beings, can also be counted among the beings of earth, because earth is part of the cosmic wholeness. In this case too, it is important to distance oneself from the usual image of angels. Rather than diaphanous winged creatures with a taste for music, they should be imagined as fields of cosmic consciousness that penetrate the entire universe. They more often reveal themselves to our perception through scents and perfumes than through form.

This list of earth's league of beings, composed of elemental beings, minerals, plants, animals, humans and angels, is still incomplete because humans lead a kind of double life. On the one hand we are incarnate on the material plane, but on the other we lead a spiritual mode of life as immortal souls. It is a fact that near the physical locations on the earth's surface that are the habitat of humans made of bone and blood, there are also etheric spaces inhabited by human souls. These may be found both in a level of the inward space of earth and in one of the invisible dimensions within the atmosphere. Some of these spaces are linked by soul pathways to form a unified, richly ramified space organism. Included are doorways through which it is possible to communicate with the so-called 'realm of ancestors'. Lastly, it should be emphasised that this earth's league of beings is an open system. At the very least we should count among their number certain beings that Earth has now and then invited here to be her guests, our extraterrestrial sisters and brothers.

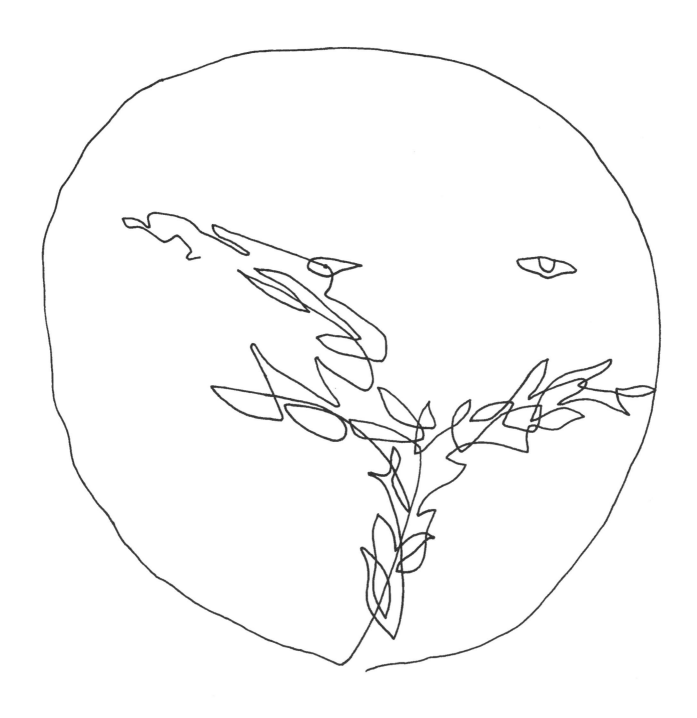

Elemental being of a plant.

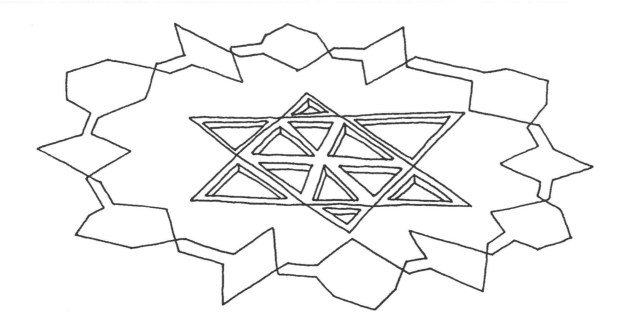

Crop circle that appeared on the 24th July, 2005,

in the immediate proximity of the Avebury stone circle.

The Avebury stone circle in England is so big that during the Middle Ages a whole village was constructed in the midst of it. Unfortunately, many of the gigantic monoliths composing the stone circle were broken up to serve as building material. We may ask how it was that Stone Age man was so extravagant of his resources as to build such a shrine. The question puzzles us because we are members of a civilization that thinks that the only things the earth can give us are the raw materials for our industry, and tourist type landscapes to enjoy.

In that far distant time humans were interested in quite different things, for example, in a closer relationship with the Earth Cosmos. 'Relationship' does not merely mean orientation in space and time. Relationship includes a constant communication that enables a person to sense the meaning of their life and steer in the direction of its fulfilment. Other than food and sexual intercourse, what else does one need to be happy?

Past peoples have sought out locations where, by the nature of the landscape, conversation runs freely between the inward space of earth's centre and the universe of the stars. They were sufficiently sensitive to find such places, which nowadays we call power points, or more accurately, chakras of the earth. In such places they built stone circles or other kinds of holy shrine to be resonance spaces that can so greatly amplify the conversation between heaven and earth that it may be experienced (as audible) by the commonality of humans.

For example, the stone circle at Avebury has been built on a power point that can be compared with our larynx chakra. To fashion the resonance space so as to sufficiently amplify the subtle vibrations of the location, it was surrounded by a high rampart set above a deep ditch. The power of the Yin-Yang polarization between the two rings enabled the erection of a light dome that originally spanned the entire area, thereby protecting the resonance space. Because of the destruction of much of the rampart area, nowadays it exists only in part.

The rituals that were performed there have prepared every one of the stones in that giant ring to be the home of an elemental being. The megaliths were thereby enlivened and can serve as agents to transmit the messages of Heaven and the Earth Soul to human beings. Within the above-mentioned resonance space it became possible to perceive their mute voice. Neolithic stone circles are not monuments, but communication tools.

Over the last two decades we have witnessed another kind of communication, which is particularly active around Avebury. Year after year, crop circles appear that are sometimes so perfect that they take the visitor's breath away. The accurate geometrical arrangement of the crop circles, whose symbolism stems from the most diverse spectrum of cultures, suggests that they too are a communication tool. One feels that beyond doubt they contain a message. Crop circles are unlike stone circles, for when genuine they are not made by human hands but created in a dance where Heaven and Earth are the dancers. The rare eyewitnesses report seeing a whirlwind that dances as fast as lightning through the field to lay down the form of the cosmogram. Scientific reports confirm that the cells of the flattened haulms are extended, not broken. It would appear that the forces of the inward earth and the consciousness of heaven are working together to translate the message of the crop circles into visible forms.

Are earth and heaven aware that modern humans cannot hear their word if it is not translated into visible forms? Stone circles and crop circles are two kinds of conversation carried on between earth, humanity and the cosmos. In form, the speech of the stone and crop circles are similar, but with one essential difference. Stone circles were erected to create a resonance space through which humans could communicate with the consciousness of the Earth Cosmos. Crop circles come into being to address the consciousness of humankind and gradually prepare us for a new level of communication within the ecosphere of earth – a communication in which the earth, cosmos and human beings become equal partners.

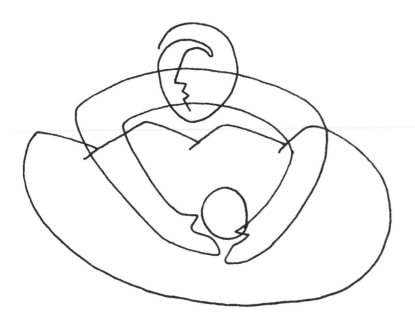

Exercise 7, to help the perfection
of locations and landscapes to manifest

Decide what you want to work with, location, landscape, river or ocean.

In the depths of the location, landscape, etc. that you have chosen lies the ball wherein its perfection is encoded.

Imagine that you reach your hands deep into the earth and enter into the midst of the chosen place, landscape, etc.

There you will find the ball of its perfection. Grasp the ball with both hands and bring it to the surface of the earth.

There open it, and let the contents flow out over the whole location (landscape, etc.), so that the area can be supported by the memory of its perfection.

Exercise 8, to soften rigid personal mental structures

Stand upright with straddled feet and outstretched hands. Position your fingers so as to make a barrier that will prevent your head falling to the floor when it rolls.

Imagine that your head is a ball of light.

Let the ball of light roll slowly along your arm, first in one direction, then in the other, till the ball of light is once again identical with your head.

It is recommended that you repeat the exercise a few times.

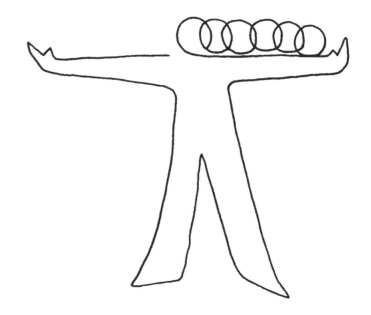

Energetic Drawing 4

The angel of the rhythms of time.

13. The End of Time

Nowadays we think of the linear time structure that rules our watches, calendars, and freedoms as being normal. The global economy would be unthinkable if we did not all accept the same time principle. Politicians pronounce on policies for the next ten years, athletes rival each other over fractions of a second. In the process we scarcely notice that linear time is a lying fairy tale told by the intellect. An abstract structure has been developed based on an acute observation of life cycles, and in the process has been objectified and nearly completely removed from its natural underpinnings. And now, though time itself is only an invention of the human intellect, we still run wildly after it, as if scared we will miss the train

Before they were constrained into the intellectual structures of linear time, earth's different cultures knew their own time rhythms. The northern winter and the southern monsoon always return at rhythmic intervals. The sun rises and sinks. Stars cross the nighttime sky and always return to their original places. This sort of cumulative experience gave rise to the idea of steady movement through cyclical time, which found expression in recurrent celebrations and initiation rituals. Now the archaic cultures, children of cyclical time, have nearly disappeared. And yet we are still alerted by the leftovers of their feeling for time. Birthdays, marriage celebrations and masses for the dead are all capable of quickly piercing the unruffled surface of linearly structured time.

Our life nowadays is a chaotic mixture of linear and cyclical time. Have we arrived at the end of time, as suggested by the Mayan calendar whose voice is silent after the year 2012? One can no longer overlook the fact that time is becoming ever shorter. One can hardly look round before a week is already past. On the other hand, one may experience time as possessing an illogical amplitude and spaciousness. When something happens that is in harmony with cosmic rhythms or the truth of being, one can get the feeling that time is filled to overflowing. Experiences can then last infinitely long. Life can draw an endless supply of time from the storehouse of eternity.

There is a third category of time that needs attention – creative time. The phrase 'the third time' is simplistic. Time is an extension of the creative phase of the universe. The eternity of being is the well that supplies the amount of time. Just as eternity is infinite, so can a single second be infinitely extended. It can happen with the experience of love, or a creative act. In such a moment we become aware that time can transcend the rigid boundaries of linear chronology. Time is free to embody the depth and breadth of our creative deeds, providing of course that they are genuine. Time becomes a dimension of our being and doing. It can manifest as much time as is needed. To suffer from a shortage of time indicates that a person has neglected either their creativity or their concordance with the force-streams of life.

As part of the process of earth transformation, the planetary soul is busy freeing herself from the patterns and constraints imposed on her by the estranged civilization of the immediate past and present. In consequence, the old temporal structures will be gradually dissolved. Simultaneously, the advantages of creative time will be offered for everyday use.

The advantages of creative time are beyond praise. You cannot tap into it if you are not wholly dedicated to your project. The creative aspect of time can neither be fooled nor sold. If we want to continue enjoying an abundance of life and time, it is required that we liberate ourselves from alienated structures of thinking and working. Otherwise, it can happen that we become a sacrifice to the time that is fast draining away. The spatial-temporal cage is getting ever narrower. Simultaneously, earth and heaven are offering humanity a new kind of being, and also a new way of distributing time. The radiant fruits of creative time can already be enjoyed, provided that we are ready to let go of old ideas and be open to the inspiration of the moment.

If we question the popular perceptions regarding time and space, we are entitled to ask whether we humans are really the sole representative of earthly civilization. What has become of those wonderful cultures from distant epochs of which our mythic heritage sings so sweetly? An Irish fairy tale tells of the original inhabitants of Ireland, the 'Tuatha de Danann' – the people of the Goddess Danu. As a culture they have completely disappeared from the Irish landscape. As spiritual beings however, the people of the Goddess Danu are still present within the realm of their hallowed sanctuaries. Changed to a fairy folk, they continue to care through their rituals and festivals for the forgotten sacred sites.

There are stories of magnificent civilizations overwhelmed by ocean waves, Atlantis for example. Must one understand this only in a physical sense? Bring to mind that the earth's surface represents a relatively thin film of the materialised world. There are other, much more diaphanous layers of space, arranged without and within. We are speaking of the inward worlds of earth and of those others turned to 'the outside', to the broad dimensions of heaven and the related universe.

In keeping with this image, we may say that over unimaginably long periods of time there are many civilizations that have come from the star-worlds to earth's surface to undergo their experience of matter. After their cycle is accomplished, they are submerged in earth's consciousness sphere and become part of her memory. Just as a human's physical plane experiences get submerged in the person's memory, there to continue their vibrations as a spiritual reality, so also do vanished civilizations continue to live in the inward earth. Each one of them can be understood as a living experience of the Earth Soul. Thus their cultures and accomplishments have a kind of posthumous life that the Earth Soul joins to her past experiences of the wonders on earth's surface to weave her veil of wisdom.

In this connection, there is some significance in a dream I had on September 22, 2005. In the dream, we are travelling in a fancy white bus. The road is full of potholes. The driver steers too close to the right-hand edge, and the bus flips over. There is however no confusion. In this keeled-over position we continue to sit in our seats and wait tensely to see what the driver is going to do. We cannot leave the bus for all its weight is lying on the side with the doors.

One gets the feeling that we passengers represent the people of earth; we can no longer avoid the fact of earth transformation, but we still deny that the earthly ecosphere's situation is critical and screams to heaven for help. On the bus, the only door that can be opened is to the left of the driver. He solemnly opens it and jumps out to push the bus upright, but his attempt to raise the bus with his bare hands fails completely. He runs off to seek help while we passengers wait in hopes he will return with a gang of strong men. No such luck. Instead, he comes back with a small person who is barely hip-high and whose facial features are strange and scarcely human. We have grave doubts that this little man can help us out. Then something unexpected happens. The little man does not try to raise the bus and free its doors, but instead creeps down between the side of the bus and the road where it is lying to access the door at the front, which he opens downwards, towards the earth's centre.

The action can be understood to mean that the vanished civilizations that live on in the inward earth, or more precisely in the earth's memory, are ready to help humanity in its need. They have already gone through global situations of a sort that we nowadays are incapable of mastering. Their experience and garnered wisdom is at our disposal. Can we, in this very moment, summon sufficient courage to jettison our limited ideas about the earth and her inner life, and listen instead to the messages from her inward worlds? One can take the dream as confirmation that, on the part of the vanished civilizations, the door to communication is held open.

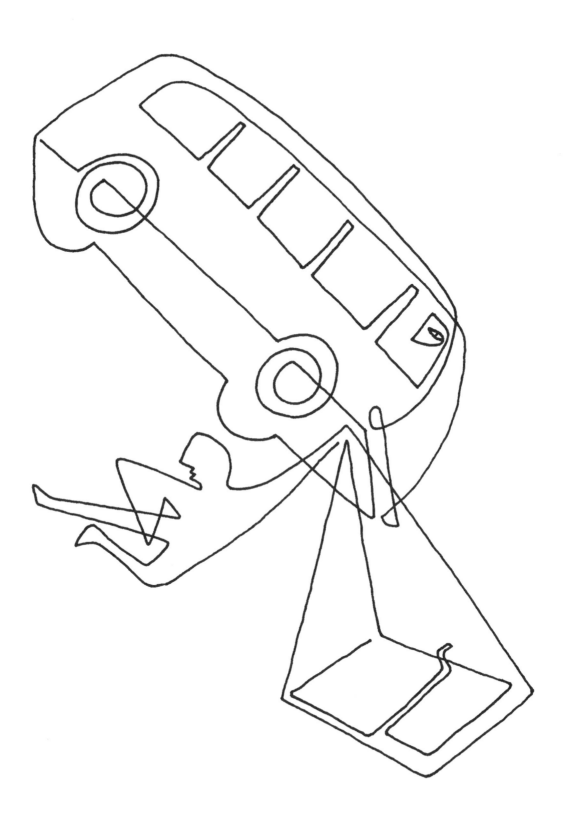

The door of the toppled bus is opened towards earth's centre.

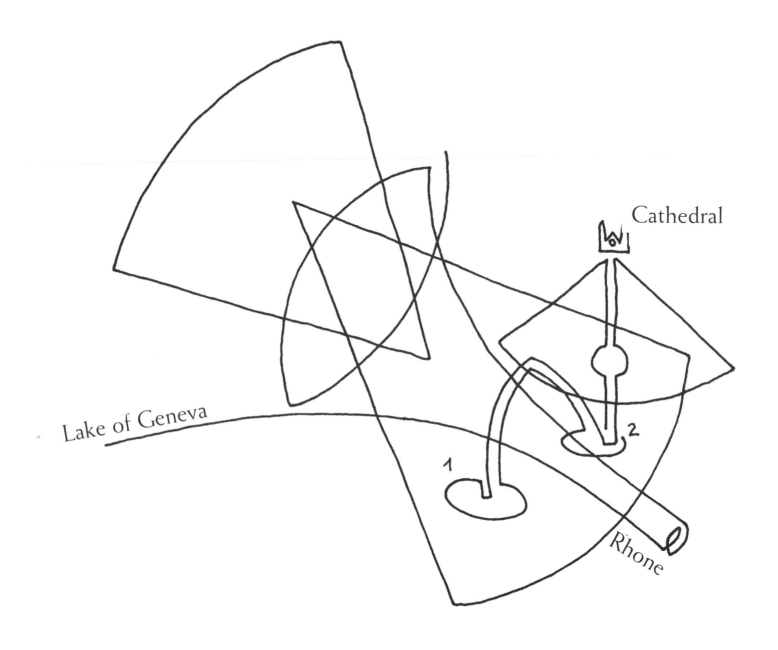

Cathedral

Lake of Geneva

Rhone

1

2

The interdimensional portal of Geneva (1=Place de Saint Gervais, 2=Place Bel-Air).

15. Geneva: Interdimensional Portals

The city of Geneva is situated at a portal of the surrounding landscape, at the point where the stillness of Lake Geneva changes to the rush and roar of the river Rhone. The town sits on low hills at the western end of the lake, and there is a gap between them that the lake has used for an exit path. The breadth of the lake is transposed into the narrowness of the river through the Geneva Gap. The word 'portal' also means, in the energetic (etheric) sense, a gap or hole through which one level or dimension of existence is translated into another: thus the material nature of the physical world is translated into the diaphanous vibrations of the inward earth.

The first question is how the portal's hole came to be. On the physical plane, it was waterpower that broke open the Geneva Gap. The likely cause was glacial action and erosion in some distant epoch. However, one cannot ascribe the formation of an etheric portal to the past; on the invisible energetic plane there exists only what is vibrating now in the given moment. Geneva's energetic portal is maintained by two pairs of opposing power focus-points, and is renewed every instant. The power focus-points are to be found on the left and right banks of the river and likewise of the lake. The right hand pillar of the river portal is located in the middle of the Place de Saint Gervais. There, deep in the earth, is a kind of disc inscribed with the portal's code. The complementary point is located on the opposite bank of the Rhone, where the Place Bel-Air debouches into the Quai Bezanson Huges. Together they act as a focus for the river nymph of the Rhone. It could be said that the code on the right-hand 'pillar' is mirrored in the consciousness of its pair on the left bank.

The second and much wider opening of the Geneva portal is anchored on opposite shores of the lake. The portal's trumpet-like opening is turned towards the lake. It lies partly below, partly above the water. The left-hand side of this second portal is located in the Parc des Eaux Vives, which is also a focus of Geneva's landscape temples. There, the form of the Triple Goddess protects the cityscape's spiritual aspect. The three aspects of the Goddess - virgin, mother and transformation - are embodied in three mighty groups of trees. On the opposite shore of the lake the portal's opening is maintained by the Parc Perle du Lac. According to tradition, the park is named for a pearl that lies deep in the Lake of Geneva and symbolises the lake's soul.

The two gateways above mentioned keep Geneva's portal open. The portal's interdimensional impact came into existence primarily through the participation of a powerful heart centre situated below the cathedral. The cathedral of St. Pierre squats on top of a pyramidal hill on whose slopes the old city of Geneva was built. Like a sun, the heart centre beams its rays into the interior of the hill. The cathedral's location is chosen such that at the intersection of its vertical and horizontal arms one can reach a vertical tunnel that leads to the light-ball of the heart centre. The vertical union between heaven and earth that one experiences thereby confirms that this place is a sanctuary of the Holy Grail.

The heart centre's green sun revolves and rhythmically unleashes an impulse that activates the operation of the interdimensional portal. The probable task of such a portal is to keep the passageway between different dimensions open in both directions. From within to the outside flow bits of information that provide the material world with the basis for its existence. The return stream carries back the temporary external bits to anchor them in the eternal wisdom of Inward Earth.

If one is looking for a corresponding phenomenon in the human being, one should consider the three light channels that connect the backspace with the manifested space of our physical body. A human being's deeds in the external world are confirmed as true by means of these three channels that connect with the archetypical space of eternity, in which we participate through our backspace. In the reverse direction, the wisdom of our broader Self (the Monad) inspires our deeds.

Exercise 9, a meditation to give yourself a taste of eternity

Imagine that your head is a ball of pure, transparent light.

Now imagine that you have indicated the crown chakra on the top of your head with a white point.

Now indicate the larynx chakra below the ball of light with a blue point.

Next, slowly turn the light-ball of your head so that the blue point rises and the white descends (as if the crown and larynx chakra are changing places).

In so doing, you have transferred the gates to the archetypical space of eternity above into your own inner space.

Now, seize the moment to open yourself to the feeling that blossoms within you. Forget the light-ball. Follow the silence.

Finally, give thanks for the experience and return to the structure of time.

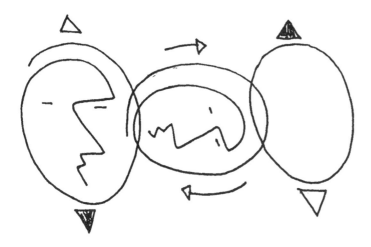

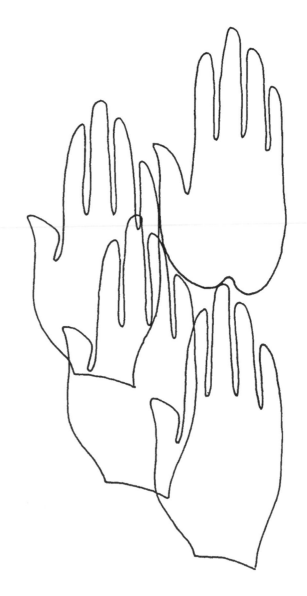

Exercise 10, to balance out heaven and earth within you (Millstones of love)

Lay one hand above the other in front of your chest, so that their edges touch.

Now begin to slowly move one hand around the other so that their edges stay in contact – like two millstones.

After a while, imagine that you are taking the grinding millstones into your heart centre. Now lead them further, deep into your backspace.

Afterwards, change the grinding direction and lead the millstones back into the space in front of you.

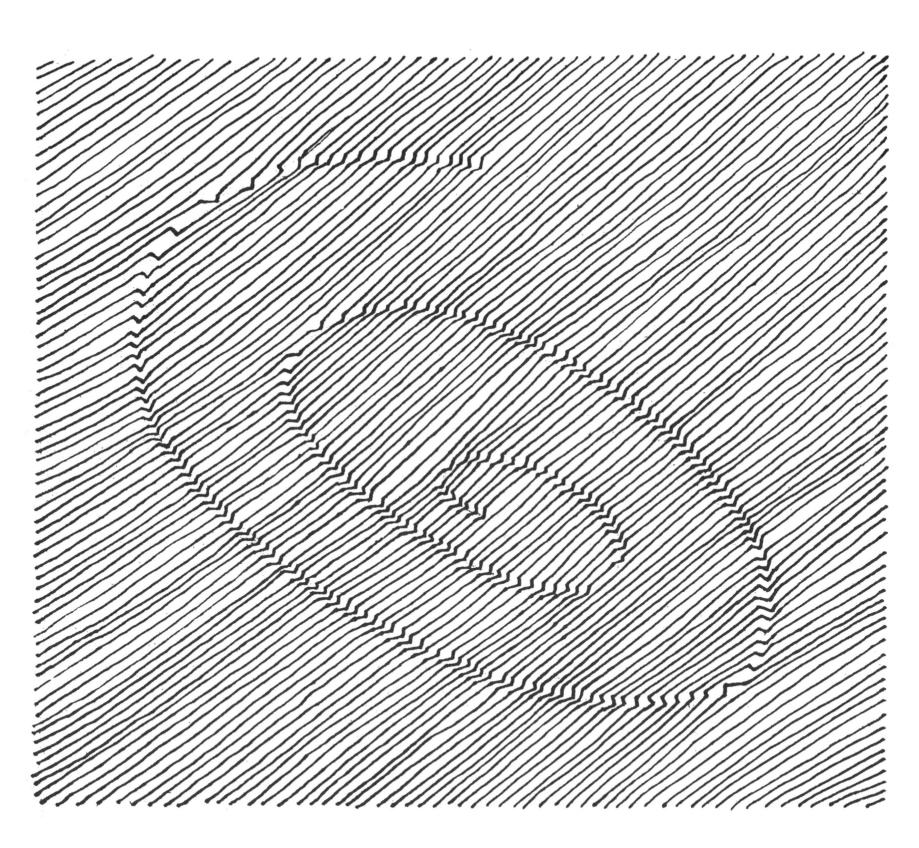

Energetic Drawing 5

The positioning and operation of the Maltese temples with reference to the human body.

16. Malta: Roots of Creation

From a child's viewpoint, father does things one way and mother does them another; so there is the way of the father and the way of the mother. Our civilization, which arose after the last ice Age, chose the way of the mother first. Thus, the Neolithic Goddess culture was created and experienced. The Archipelago of Malta is one of the places where the memory of the Goddess culture is most richly preserved. The pelvic area of the human body is another place that holds the memory of the Goddess culture. If one follows the way of the father, the cosmos expresses itself through our head area, above all through the larynx. The language of the father is the word. In contrast, the impulse of the Goddess finds its expression through the pelvic area, through the belly region centred in the navel. The Goddess speaks through the eternal, self-renewing life.

Who does not know of the Maltese Goddess figures with their broad hips, so upsetting to modern fashion? In many instances their tiny heads are missing, so one gets the impression that the thinking of these mighty women revolves within the 'skull' indicated by their pelvic bones. The sphere of thinking was not yet separated from the sphere of being. However, it would be wrong to suggest that the Goddess Culture must have moved exclusively along the wheel of metabolism and sexuality. Quite the opposite! That centring deep in the pelvis makes it possible for the universal spirit to be even more thoroughly embodied in matter than is customary among us nowadays.

The spiritual impulse that created the global culture of the Goddess originates in the realm of the earth's centre. Its openness to the inspirations of the Earth Soul and her cosmic wisdom allows a consciousness model of the paradisiacal world to be created in the pelvic chalice of each member of the Goddess Culture and, projected to the outside, it was lived from generation to generation. The famous megalithic temples of Gozo and Malta are obviously constructed on the model of the pelvic chalice. If you lie down, you can compare their form to your own pelvic region. Now you have the depths of the earth at your back and the sphere of heaven arches above the vault of your stomach. You are anchored in earth's centre on one side and, on the other, open to heaven. This is precisely how the Maltese temples are constructed, so that messages from the heavens can be perceived and interpreted.

Like a perfectly calm sea the water of eternal life ascends from the earth's centre up to the base of the megalithic temple and acts as a mirror that reflects the messages of the universe. The function of the rituals that took place there was probably to perceive the experience of the heavenly messages and move them upwards, towards the head. Something of this, lived from day to day, was invested through the service in the temple in the construction of the individualized humanity of the future. If you lie down on your back and then stand upright, you can comprehend the ritual function of the temple.

The heads of the Maltese Goddesses, which were fastened to the sculpted pieces, are much too small in proportion to their bodies and symbolise the embryo of the free and independent human being, at that time still a closely guarded mystery. It is hypothesised that the heads were only fastened to the bodies in particular rituals. And now here we are, human beings that were then still in the future, centred in our heads and egocentrically oriented. Have we become a realisation of the vision that was nurtured in the megalithic temples of Malta millennia ago?

We are now experiencing the shadow side of the development that has brought us from the paradisiacal model conceived in the pelvis to the iron rule of the head. The connecting umbilical cord has meanwhile withered. In the defiled and tourist-beleaguered temples of Malta is encoded the memory of that umbilical cord that can connect a horizontal lying person with heaven and earth. In one's own practice, one can refer to the lumbar channel, a light channel that joins the earth's centre to the breadth of heaven through our pelvic region. To follow its course, you should imagine a person lying horizontally. The sex chakra works with the solar plexus and triangulates with a back chakra located below the sacrum to raise the channel's vibration.

Exercise 11, to experience
the qualities of the lumbar channel

1. *Lie down on your back and stretch yourself out.*

2. *Imagine — and above all feel — that you are lying on the surface of a sheet of water that is totally calm.*

3. *You now construct a bridge of light that leaves your larynx area and goes up and around your head towards your backspace.*

4. *Imagine yourself tiny and running over the bridge and down your back till you reach the level of your sacrum.*

5. *There you find a radiant light door. Go through it into your abdominal space and look about you.*

6. *Sense the quality of the space between the hips, and how the relationships with the heavens and earth's centre replenish themselves.*

7. *Lastly, bring the essence of the experience into your upper body, so that it can become active there.*

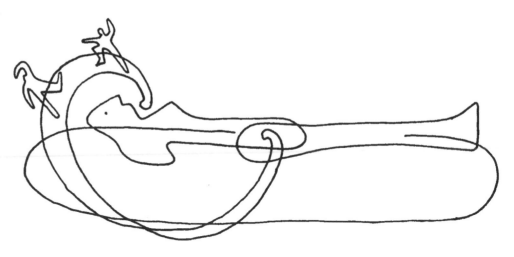

Exercise 12, The Malta prayer position:
speak with the Goddess within you

1. *Lay your hands in your lap and cross your fingers so that you make a chalice in your lap.*

2. *Ask that the Goddess (or your soul) fill the chalice with her presence or message.*

3. *Without letting go of the chalice, you should now raise your hands towards your heart area. In so doing, put your hands together as in prayer, so that your two hands form the ball of divine perfection.*

4. *In the usual prayer position you cross your thumbs, so that they close off the inner space of the ball. Now you should consciously push them aside, so that the door is open to the temple of the Goddess.*

5. *Now begins the intimate conversation with the soul of the universe, heart to heart, and its most important component is the exchange of feelings.*

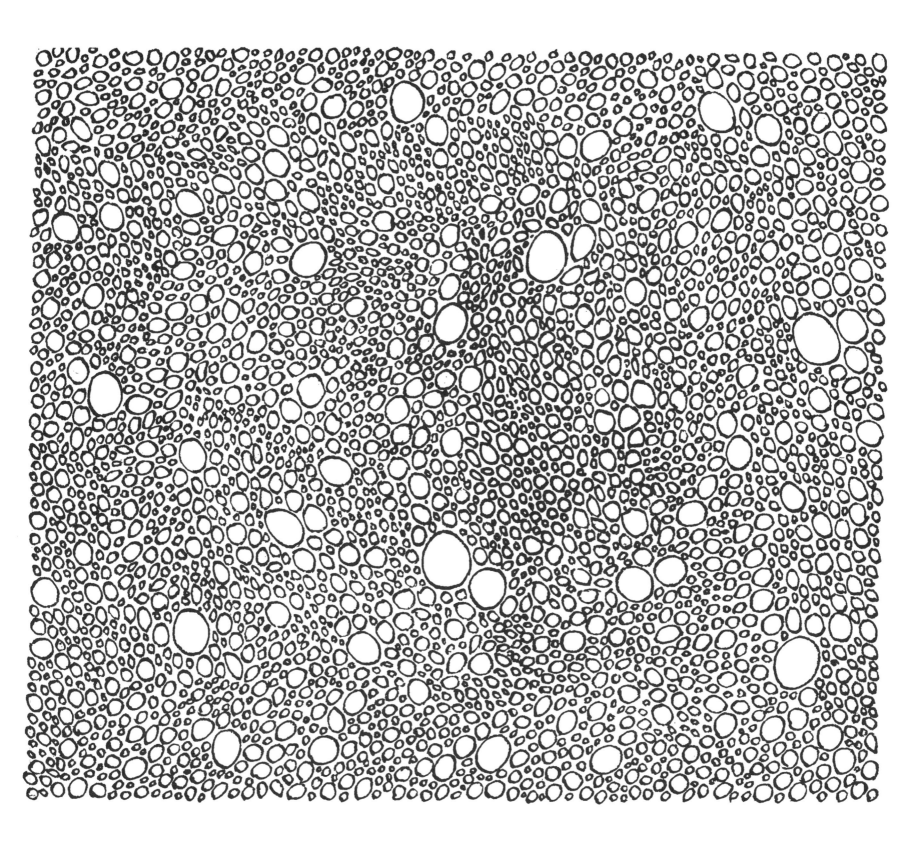

Energetic Drawing 6

17. Seeland, Switzerland: Landscape of the Ensouled Earth

We humans are in the habit of seeking out different vocations to give some meaning to our lives. The universe contains beings whose chosen profession is to vivify a planet. Such a profession is not as quickly discarded as the human sort. This raises the question, how one should name the enlivening being of the planet earth. The ancient Greeks proposed 'Gaia'; in Latin, the corresponding name is 'Terra'. If juxtaposed with the human constitution, then Terra /Gaia is the soul of planet earth. Before the planet could be enlivened, a cosmic being had to decide to ensoul the earth, which is to say, embody itself in the earth.

Rather than spin intellectual theories, we should ask how we can perceive the ensoulment and subsequent enlivenment of the earth in an actual landscape. The concept of ensoulment suggests that life's radiation is projected from within to the outside. The material veil is illumined from within, and one can discern from the surface of a human body that it is emitting the impulse of life. So what can someone on the earth's surface discern from the luminosity of the landscape? Just as the sun spreads its light in the visible landscape, so does the earth. The difference is that the emission from Gaia is much finer and therefore appears invisible. What are its traits? First, one can perceive the radiation of the Earth Soul as ground radiation on the earth's surface. We are speaking here of different force fields that penetrate the material landscape. Second, one can discern the conscious enlivenment of the earth by the power organism that passes through the landscape. We are looking at a composition of power centres (chakras) and power highways (ley-lines) that serve as life organs for the earth's surface. They are responsible for providing the landscape with the powers and qualities that we all, landscape organisms and beings of the surface too, need to fulfil our life's role and so be able to evolve.

The composition of the landscape temple on the earth's crust represents a third aspect of the ensouled earth. This is the spiritual plane of the landscape, through which the Earth Soul reveals herself directly and without intermediary. In line with the principle 'as without, so within', the Earth Soul is mirrored on her surface through the different forms of landscape temples.

And because a holographic fragment of the Godhead dwells within every soul, we may speak of the landscape temples of the Goddess. Of course, we are not dealing here with any buildings, because the existing forms of the landscape have themselves developed into a temple structure. They are worked by Earth's own modelling hands – for example by glaciers or erosion – and are usually overbuilt with the sacred buildings of different cultures.

The landscape temple of the Swiss Seeland is divided nearly symmetrically into two units. They are separated by a relatively low mountain ridge, which gives rise to two oblong depressions. In the northern depression, which runs beside the Jura Mountains, lie the Lac de Bienne and further west, the Lac de Neuchatel. The southern depression is designated by the Lac de Morat, which to the east merges into the Great Moss of earlier times.

The landscape temple of the northern depression (Lac de Bienne) is dedicated to the light aspect of the Goddess, the southern in contrast to the dark, night aspect (the Great Moss). The light aspect of the landscape temple is arranged and indicated by a clear long-axis. Like a line of chakras, the axis begins to gather its power in La Thene, on the eastern shore of the Lac de Neuchatel. The archetypical power of the earth is concentrated there, as in the root chakra for humans. Like a dragon, this archetypical power snakes its way into the middle of the Lac de Bienne, to Peter's Island. This is the brightest, most light-filled point in the whole of Seeland. A vertical axis is centred on Peter's Island, which binds together two mighty light pyramids. One points to the heavens, the other is turned downwards to earth's centre. They are placed there to balance the relationship between heaven and earth.

In contrast, the dark aspect of the landscape temple displays no such geometrical layout. Rather it portrays a constant dance of the qualities that stimulate the transformation from death to rebirth.

Cosmogram of the light (on left) and dark (on right) aspects of Seeland's landscape temple.

Exercise 13, for balancing the light and dark (invisible) aspects of the body

Stand upright with legs somewhat apart.

Imagine that your head is identical to a ball of light.

Let the ball roll slowly down along your back. Make sure that it is constantly touching the body's surface.

When the ball reaches the base of the vertebral column, bring it forwards between your legs.

Now slowly roll it upwards over the anterior side of the body till it is once again united with your head.

It is recommended that you repeat the exercise several times.

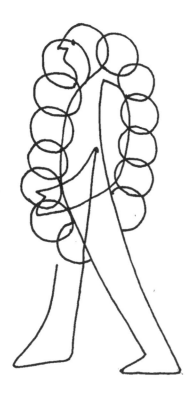

Exercise 14, to bring the archetypical powers of the back towards the front, so that they may be better integrated in creative processes. (Holographic gesture from Basle)

You are standing up. Hold your hands together behind your back in such a way that the middle fingers touch your buttocks. Imagine that you have a tail that reaches to the middle of the earth to join you with earth's archetypical power.

Now slowly raise your arms to draw the archetypical power of the earth up the anterior length of your body till it reaches the larynx. This will establish the connection between the archetypical power of the earth and your own personal creative potency.

Bend your head backwards to symbolically open your larynx chakra.

Now let your hands glide outwards from the larynx so that their creative potency is opened to the outer world.

You should repeat the gesture a few times.

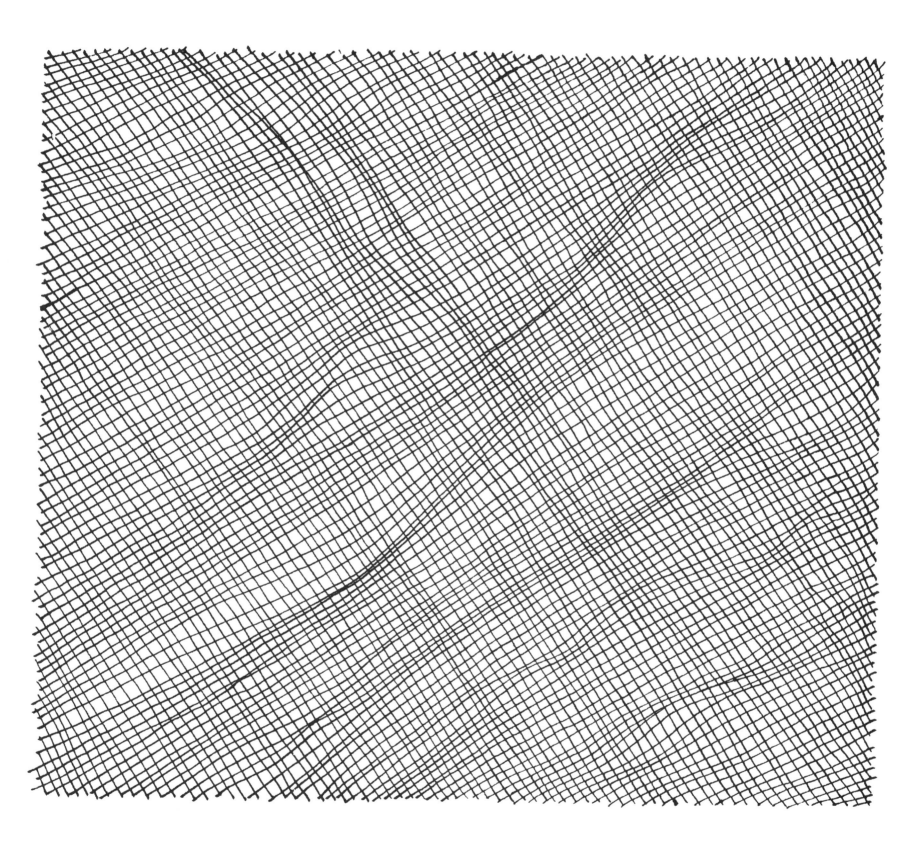

Energetic Drawing 7

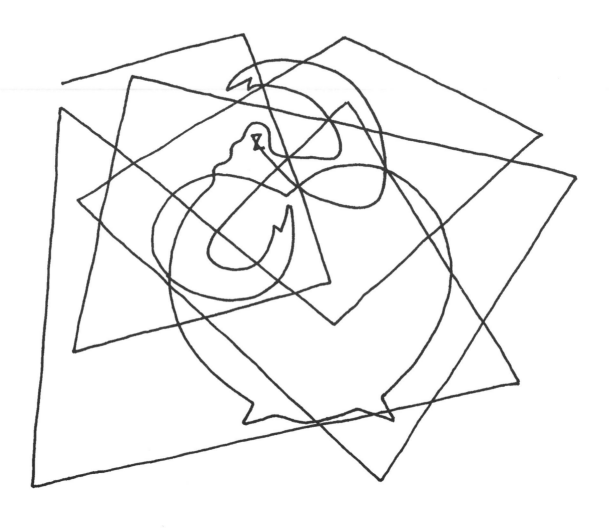

The earth is strong enough to liberate itself from the patterning that has been imposed on it.

18.   Storms on the Emotional Plane

The present civilization is able to race so fast towards the future because it is driven by our individualised intellect. This is no secret. Said differently, the logical intellect has broken off from the rest of the Wholeness, enabling humanity to acquire for itself fantastic opportunities to move through space and time. It is almost unbelievable, the number of new things that intellect conjures up daily! It is difficult for the other parts of our Wholeness to keep up. So it happens that a civilization that splits hairs to establish specific human rights will simultaneously develop terrible weapons of mass destruction - and even be ready to use them.

It should be obvious that the speed at which the intellect and its whole court of scientific knowledge are racing towards a completely unknown future is in no way healthy for a person's inner balance. It is relatively easy for the head to conquer new horizons. The opposite is true of the abdomen, treasure chamber of the emotions, which moves much more slowly. Time and patience are needed to work through the feelings associated with events and to ground them through experience.

The distorted balance between belly and head finds expression in the division of modern man, who on the one hand is intoxicated by the light of intelligence, and on the other suffers in the darkness of cramped emotional restraints. This fateful inner division expresses itself on the world scene as a distressful separation between those who enjoy exaggerated wealth and those who are the traumatic sacrifice of war and starvation.

But let us not think that intellect is evil in itself! Logical thinking is the guarantee of our freedom to choose, create and love. Also, the emotional worlds are no pure gold mine. How easy it is to get burnt by egocentric ambition or blind devotion! One should position oneself in the balance between the two extremes. Then the question would be how to imbue the forces of the intellect with love for the wholeness of life; and how to ground the forces of the emotions through our conscious, ethically guided decisions. Because the balance of humanity is upset and Earth's balance thereby threatened, we have become witness to ever more frequent natural catastrophes. Earth is striving towards a new balance by unleashing the elemental forces. We are speaking of the four elements, and primarily of the elemental beings that are their emotional consciousness.

Earthquakes (element earth), storms (air), volcanic eruptions (fire) and floods (water) are not only shocking events that evoke strong human emotions, but also forms of conscious emergency assistance in circumstances that could otherwise let loose a world-ending cataclysm. Unfortunately, they are linked to so much sacrifice that we come to catharsis nonetheless. Dammed up emotions are suddenly stirred into movement. The ice of the enchained emotional fields is temporarily broken.

The storms on the emotional plane are best understood as unwished-for emergency assistance. To prevent the danger of a total ossification of the world organism, the energetic forces were temporarily coupled with the emotional. We humans really had to rack our brains to dream up a state of emergency like this! Because the energetic plane has been coupled with the emotional, difficulties that torment a person's feelings can present immediate health problems; often ones for which no logical explanation can be found.

On the other hand, this unpleasant coupling gave us humans the chance to help directly in the emergency effort to rebalance the Earth. We give such help every time our thoughts are consciously balanced by the feeling of wholeness. We help every time we soften the logical and stressful impact of our deeds through heart-felt laughter. Things have gone so far between earth and humanity that it is no longer possible to avoid a dramatic situation on the emotional plane. It is however possible to kick the bottom out of the whole cumulative barrel of frustrated and negatively oriented emotions.

19. Deliverance from the Pattern of Force

Do not rejoice overmuch that European wars are a thing of the past! Right now, all over the world, thousands of young people are playing on their computers and trying to eliminate their hideous opponents. Hundreds and thousands more are sitting in the football stadiums to experience the stubborn battles of their favourite teams. And what of the hidden fight between the sexes, carried on behind the window shutters of innumerable living rooms? Force often repeats itself although, seek you far and wide, no grounds are to be found. Not long ago we were rejoicing over politicians who were campaigning for world peace, and already warmongers have replaced them. Everything seems to be sliding downhill to damnation.

But that is not true! We are dealing with the logical consequences of the repetition of a single pattern that follows a twisted archetype buried deep in the human psyche. Still worse: this unlucky pattern is not confined to one level, for its metastases hide on different planes of our emotional fields, mental ideas and even of our genetic data. This is the pattern that force takes. It is a pattern of loveless polarization, of craving for power, of cold-hearted contact with those nearest you, of competitive attitudes and bellicose arguments. It is stamped deep in our genes, as if mixed in our blood. It is sleeping within us, but can be reactivated at any instant, sometimes as an innocent prankster, at other times as a grisly murderer.

How does it happen that we repeatedly fall victim to this falsification of the basic ground of our being? To begin to heal, one should view distorted patterns of this sort as a cosmic challenge. It may be that humanity has inherited them from previous civilizations that destroyed themselves by a stiff-necked attachment to the patterns of force. But the most important question is not how the pattern originated. It is more important to view the distorted pattern as a creative opportunity.

The pattern of force is a shadow aspect of love: if we are incapable of embodying the fragrant quality of love, we become prey to, and eaten up by, the pattern of force; if we are incapable of dealing with one another lovingly and cooperatively, we get embroiled in wars and all other kinds of altercation. However,

the opposite is also true: if a person can maintain a correct and affectionate relationship in a situation, the 'demon of force' is overcome and peace is free to extend its own force field. The best outcome is to replace the distorted pattern in oneself whilst living in positive contrast. Such might be the educative meaning of the suffering imposed by the pattern of force that has accompanied human history through millennia.

To free oneself from the pattern of force is quite a different thing. Let us assume that the earth is changing and wants to develop a space that is free of force. Humanity is therefore challenged to free itself from this genetically based, destructive model. In general, is that possible?

The World Soul has planned that the solution to this question should take the form of the redeemer. We speak here of a divine being that is so pure that it can enter the destructive pattern without being affected by it. A redeemer is even capable of embodying the distorted archetype and thereby transforming it into light. Western culture knows one example of a redeemer's blessed work in the crucifixion and resurrection of Jesus Christ. The 14 stages of the so-called 'Way of the Cross' signify different phases of the redeemer's entrance into the oppressive pattern of force. He was betrayed, spat upon, beaten and lastly crucified with criminals. Instead of defending himself and demonstrating his divine supremacy, he gave the pattern full rein to vent all its aggression right into the abyss of death. Christ's resurrection symbolises the fateful pattern's transformation into light, by which it has potentially lost its power over us humans. Like a wave of the sea, the redemption spreads out through space and time.

Then how is it that we still nowadays suffer from the pressure of this destructive pattern? The Bible addresses this question when it speaks of men's hardened hearts, and in contrast, of the opening of the heart. For as long as people's hearts remain hardened, the wave of redemption cannot reach them. We cannot avoid opening our hearts in order to free ourselves effectively from the pattern of force.

When a human heart opens itself to the wave of redemption.

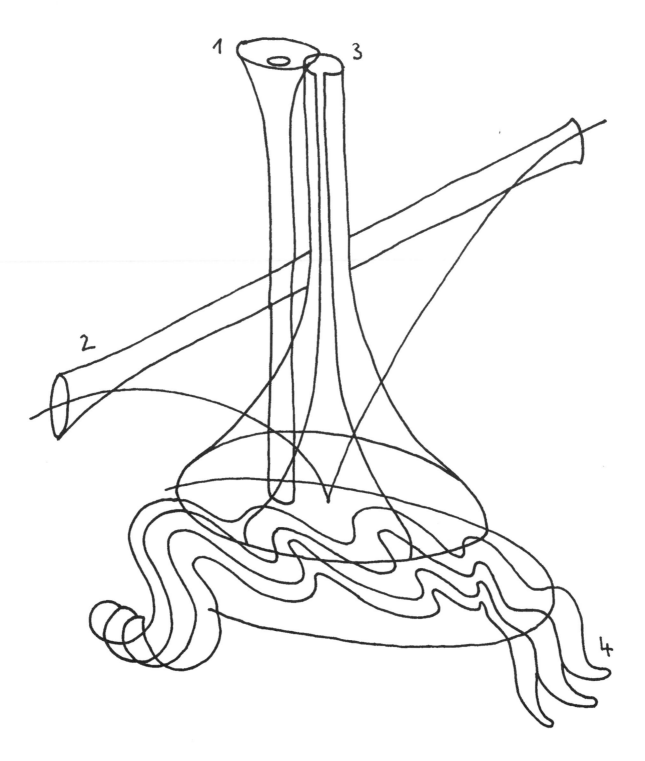

A cosmic matrix is impressed on the water at Paderborn

1 = angelic focus on the Bartholomew Chapel,

2 = aerial (atmospheric) power highway,

3 = focus of the spiritual world,

4 = the springs at Paderborn

20. Paderborn, Germany: Healing, Holy Water

There is a town at the source of the river Pader. It is called Paderborn. A limestone slab covering the local landscape ends suddenly in a hillside slope in the midst of the town. Streams of water running beneath the slab burst out into the light of day. Water from the earth's interior shoots out from many springs. In Paderborn water is born. Water is a fluid crystal with a capacity for memory far exceeding silicon. A stream of water that flows from the earth naturally brings with it information regarding the elemental forces. The atomic structure of water is pervaded with life force. But something else is happening to the springs at Paderborn. Before the water there sees the bright daylight, it is intensely irradiated by cosmic forces. Each drop of water comes impressed with a cosmic seal.

This impression takes place shortly before the water leaves the nether world. At the site of this powerful cosmic irradiation stands the cathedral and nearby, the Chapel of St. Bartholomew. Whence comes this mighty irradiation? One can count three cosmic sources that, as if by chance, are thrusting against each other over the site. One of them is an aerial power highway (ley-line) that runs through the atmosphere and is part of the network of cosmic ley-lines. It ties the Arctic with the Atlantic Ocean and its course runs through Lapland, Paderborn, Montsegur in the Pyrenees, and Gibraltar. The second has to do with a focus of angelic consciousness that is centred in the chapel of St. Bartholomew. Built in the 11th century by Byzantine masters, one is almost aghast at its unbelievable acoustics. The third aspect concerns the world of the ancestors, which is usually labelled the 'spiritual world'. It takes the form of an 'etheric city' that vibrates above the local landscape and has its gateway near Paderborn's cathedral.

These are the three components of the cosmic seal that impress their qualities on the water of Paderborn. The interaction between water and the cosmic seal could be compared with the wedding between heaven and earth. The water's elemental earthly essence is coupled with the threefold cosmic irradiation at the very instant before it opens itself to the light of day. As the original peoples would say, 'Mother Earth' and 'Father Heaven' have sexual intercourse there. Myth would tell of the 'sacred wedding'.

Let us put myth to one side. What is really happening? We are looking at a synthesis that enables life to unfold in physical form. A body is being prepared for the instreaming forces of heaven. One can also see it the other way about: the body of water is ensouled by cosmic impulses. In fact, one can perceive an unexpected wealth of elemental beings stepping out of the strongly ensouled waters of the springs. There is a legend that tells of a paradisiacal world lying below the cathedral of Paderborn: 'in that place there is a land with palaces built of precious rock, from which stairways lead ever deeper into ever more magnificent rooms; gardens spread out before you, in which diamond flowers are blooming and brooks ripple with liquid silver...' Obviously this describes a medial form between the glory of the spiritual world and the life force of its earthly counterpart. The world that comes into being through the marriage of heaven and earth is simultaneously grounded in the sense of scenic landscape imbued with supernatural beauty.

Such will not come to pass on earth if human beings remain unready to open themselves to the synthesis of earth and heaven, which is anchored in everyday reality by our relationships and deeds. Truth is that this possibility exists only when one has determined to lay aside all egocentric desires and devote oneself fully to the synthesis of spirit and life force within one's own being. In the instant that one achieves this, the cosmic seals of the water of Paderborn are opened and they begin to pour out their sacred message.

Exercise 15, to open your heart
to the wave of redemption

Imagine that you are standing inside a spacious light-ball that symbolises the forces of redemption.

Let your feelings vibrate with the urgent wish that the blessings of redemption should saturate the light-ball.

Now begin the process of opening your heart. You start in the area of the sex organs, where most genetic information is stored. From there, raise your attention vertically towards the heart centre.

Once you have reached the level of the heart, begin to open the body's interior space to the outside, like a ball turned inside out. What is inside begins to stretch itself out around you and is turned to the outside.

Remain within the inverted sphere of your being and let it be irradiated by the sun of the redeemer. It is as if you are exposing your own interior to ventilation and irradiation by the divine ball within which we find ourselves.

Afterwards, follow the curve of the ball back into your heart, and all parts of your being are thereby returned to their original places.

Give thanks for the sphere of the redeemer through which the destructive pattern is absorbed and transformed. This exercise should be repeated several times in the following days, for as long as you feel it necessary.

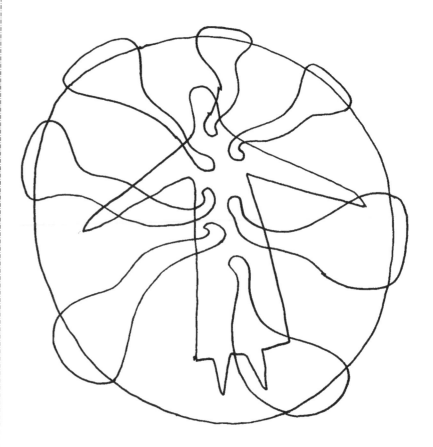

Exercise 16, to free oneself momentarily from
the dominion of the intellectual self (ego)

Be conscious of the celestial sphere around you.

In the silence, ask the network of your external self to pause for a moment, so that you may be free of its control while you make decisions, perceive, etc.

Imagine that, as quick as lightning, you pull the network out of your bodily structure and hang it on various points of the sphere that surrounds you.

Now that you have won some moments of freedom, use them as planned. Your freedom will probably last but a short while, for we still need the ego to be able to function in the old time structure.

If for example one is in a forest, one can also ask an experienced tree to hold the structure of the ego for a few moments.

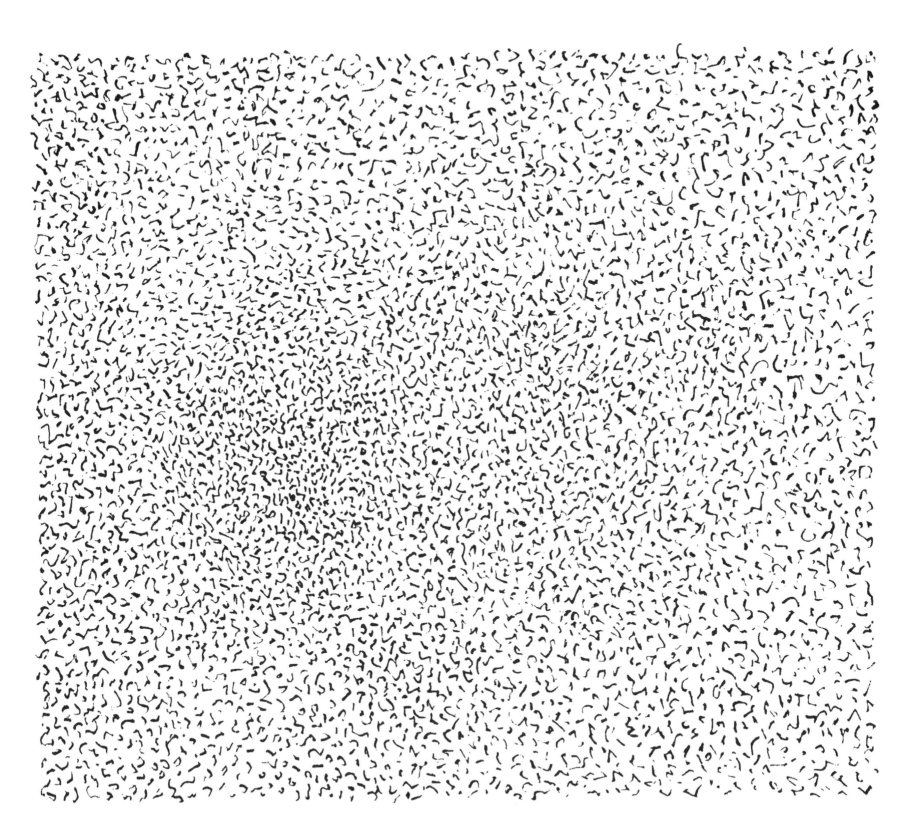

Energetic Drawing 8

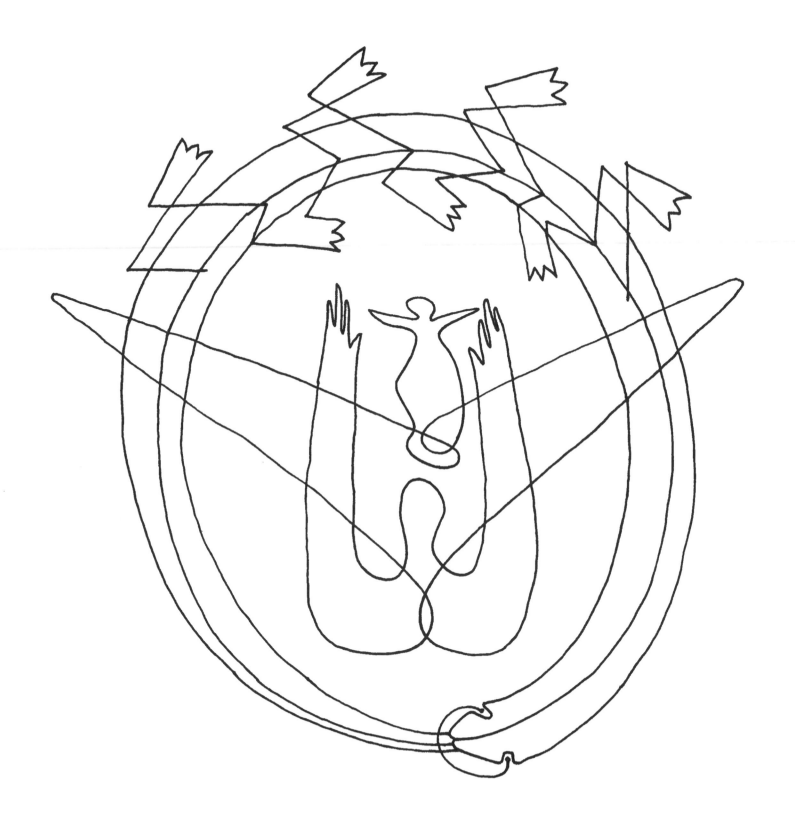

The Virgin of the Apocalypse has born a child in the face of the cosmic dragon.

21.   A Revolution in Heaven

In a wider sense we can see the universe as our home. It is our own place. So we are naturally interested in what goes on in heaven. However, there is no TV channel to report on that! We find our best information in the Revelation of St. John – the book that is also called the Apocalypse. In symbolic language, this reports on a revolution in heaven. The key statements are to be found in the exact centre of the book, in the 12th chapter. The encounter between the celestial virgin and a red dragon represents the immediate drama of what is happening in the universe.

The virgin is on the point of bearing her son who embodies a new ordering of the universe. The dragon that opposes them, called 'the old snake,' represents the organizational pattern of the world's systems that have existed until now. It rages furiously to protect its power and throne. The Apocalypse bears witness that in heaven the dispute is already decided. The old order must cede to the new. But not so on earth. Our planet has been chosen to be a kind of touchstone for the new world order. The old dragon is surely beaten, but has been permitted to land on planet earth and be active here for a short space of time. The 'democratic' constitution of the universe gives it one last chance to prove that its world system is superior to the new, represented on earth by two 'would-be revolutionaries', Buddha in the East and Christ in the West.

The creators of the new order have reserved the right to assist earth and humanity in this difficult test. The 11th chapter of the Revelation reports how two witnesses of the transformed universal order have been sent to earth. Buddha, born in the East, renounced his princely status and the religious traditions commonly held sacred. He has shown people how, through compassion for all creatures, one can withdraw from the wheel of karma and become free. In the West Christ has taught people that we are not born to serve an imposed hierarchical order. He has demonstrated through his healing miracles that within our own being there slumbers the divine power that can liberate us from death of body and spirit.

To silence the dangerous doctrines of these two messengers, powerful religious organisations were erected. Though based on their work, these often do more to preserve themselves than to embody the new archetypical mode of being. To these we may add other contrivances by which the old world order asserts itself, for example, 19th century rationalism. Humanity became enveloped in a mental structure that dooms us to separation from the forces and inspirations of multidimensional earth and the spiritual world. Its guiding concept belongs to the headlines of the old order. The human being is too immature for freedom. We need to be steered along previously prepared lines like a tram. We need to hear simple explanations from the World Being, ones that the brain can comprehend. To ensure we do not lose our way in the process, feelings of guilt must be implanted beforehand.

The controlled chaos of the consumer society was established as an alternative to the above. If people were clever enough to get out from the rationalistic pincers, they should become the prisoners of freedom. The materialist society calls for all kinds of consumer durables that have the power to lead a person away from their true being. Humans are then free to decide between innumerable negligible differences. However, one should not see the 'revolution in heaven' as a bellicose conflict between two parties. The conflict is not between me and some other, it takes place within each of earth's inhabitants. The obsolete pattern of existence confronts the new possibilities for development and evolution within every single being of the earthly cosmos. By the way, it is not possible to conquer the old order from without. Who can persuade humanity to line up on the right side if we remain completely unaware of our participation in an ongoing cosmic drama?

Let us imagine the All as a universe comprising three co-existing phases. In the first phase we have the universe of eternity, of endless peace, the universe of eternal Nirvana. The second phase brings into being solar systems, worlds and civilizations. This is the creative phase of the universe where the riches of life and civilization proliferate throughout the universe. This creative phase could lead into fragmentation, into innumerable particularities, even to a terminal alienation from the Source, if there was not potential for a third phase of the All, the phase of transformation.

Keeping a rhythmical distance from each other, waves of transformation roll through the universe. Grounded in divine compassion, they dissolve the obsolete forms and guide beings and worlds back to the Well of Being. The biblical myth of the Flood and the Ark of Noah tells of the last wave of cosmic transformation to hit the earth. The world that sank in the great flood of that time represents the old earth space, the old ecosphere, which was no longer capable of carrying humanity's evolution any further. The ship that Noah built to preserve the life of plants, animals and human beings represents the nucleus of the new earth space. This is the earth space that we, as the civilization that arose after the Flood, nowadays enjoy.

Noah's Ark is a symbol that stands for the etheric structure of the new space. The animals, humans and plants were not saved because they embarked aboard a ship. The embarkation is a symbol of rapport with the new space that assured secure foundations for a new cycle of earth evolution. It is significant that Noah's 'spacecraft' had sufficient room for all kinds of animals and plants, but only for a few humans. According to the biblical story, nearly all of humanity drowned in the waves of the great Flood. However, because the Flood had unleashed a cosmic transformation, plants and animals, being holographic entities of nature, vibrated in tune with it. They glided with the wave of transformation, to be transported onto the plane of the new earth space.

It is different for human beings: we have attained a stage of independence that does not allow us to ride 'automatically' with the wave of transformation. There is a message here for today's epoch of transformation. During an epoch of transformation, it is not enough to devote one's attention to the everyday flow of affairs. One is required to seek further. Though certainly necessary, it is not sufficient just to ensure the daily food supply, fulfil one's obligations and enjoy life. One needs to simultaneously stretch one's antennae into the regions behind the daily scenes of life. One should check again and again to trace the vibrations of the true reality, to ensure one is not confused and led astray by what is apparently real.

During a period of epochal transformation, the old space, the one without a future, does not stand aside while the new space prepares itself, like a Noah's Ark. That would allow one to choose where one wanted to be. And, when the cosmic tsunami wave came crashing, one could save oneself on the Noah's Ark, that is to say, in the new space structure. But this is not what happens. Both viewpoints of today's reality are present simultaneously. What appears as a wave of transformation approaching earth has in fact arrived long ago, for its rhythm vibrates outside time. There are two reasons why we do not notice this. First, we are too deeply frozen within the old projections and patterns to be capable of perceiving the paradisiacal quality of the new, youthful space, as fine and subtle as angel's breath. Second, the old space structure is still so sustainable that we believe ourselves embedded within secure coordinates. The human being is drunk on the apparent stability of evanescent space. True stability has nothing to do with external circumstances. True stability depends on concordance with the vibration of the eternal *now*.

Sampling the sphere of the new space.

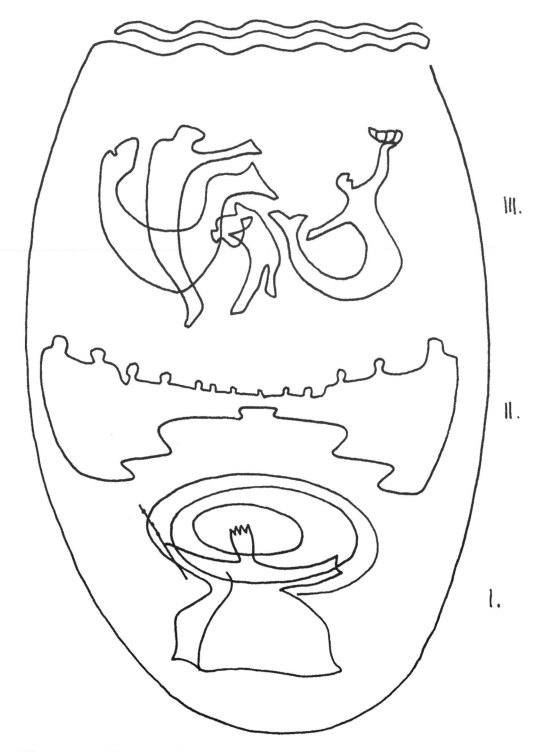

The painting 'The Triumph of Venice' by Jacopo Tintoretto as a key to paradise

I: Archetype of Paradise

II: Masters of the Archetype

III: World of Elemental Beings

IV: The Venetian Lagoon

23.   Venice: Perfume of Paradise

Whoever has visited Venice at different seasons of the year will readily agree that the watery city brings up recollections of an archetypical paradise. One might point to the city's unbelievably subtle beauty, especially true on days when a faint mist hovers in the air. One speaks of this in relation to the 'romantic Venice'. Is it possible that this 'romantic' quality has to do with the perfection of paradise, and with the matrix of the perfected earth that slumbers deep in the planet's interior? There are different possible ways of interpreting the reality of paradise. One of them holds the memory of a 'golden age', when humans still lived in harmony with plants, animals and the cosmic cycles. That memory is stored in our subconscious. It is still with us today, driving us to seek ways to end wars and realize a harmonious civilization. A second way is to imagine paradise as a consciousness layer within the earth's interior. Shamanist cultures speak of the netherworld and make reference to the archetypical world tree. Its branches reach high into the cosmos. Its trunk represents the life on the earth's surface, which we humans share with animals and plants. Its roots grip deep into the earth and touch the world of paradise.

By paradise is meant the matrix of the perfected earth that is guarded by the consciousness of the Earth Soul in the core of the planetary body. The perfection of every single being on the earth's surface is encoded therein. Actually it already lives there as a spiritual quality. We are all gradually developing in the direction of our codes that are guarded in that nether world of paradise. There are particular places on the earth's surface that resonate more strongly than others with the memory of the paradise in earth's centre. This is true of Venice, a town that stands, literally, in the water of a lagoon. It is the giant watery mirror, coupled with a complex heart system, that gives Venice that special sensibility we have noted.

The secret of Venice's relationship to the archetype of paradise is shown in a painting that is on public display in the Senate Hall of the Doge's Palace. This is the giant painting called 'The Triumph of Venice' that Jacopo Tintoretto created for the ceiling of the hall during the years 1585-95. The painting makes plain that there are three phases to the matrix of paradise. To perceive them in the correct sequence, one should view the painting from the perspective of the person who is approaching the doge's throne at the end of the hall – that is, the exact opposite of the way the image appears in books. Right below, in the midst of a fiery ball, one sees the Goddess Venice enthroned. Surrounded by seven Gods, she represents the matrix of perfection stored in the memory of the Earth Soul. Therein too is encoded the divine power through which it is possible to realize paradise on earth. If one goes a little further from earth's centre towards the surface, one reaches the layer that the painting represents as an endless row of persons who are sitting on clouds. This is a representation of the 'ancestors of paradise', spirits of bygone cultures who preserve the memory of the paradise on the earth's surface. Their experience renders them capable of inspiring and guiding the reconstruction of paradise on the earth's surface. The third phase is represented by sea nymphs and other elemental beings. Their task is to carry the impulses for the construction of the paradisiacal quality to the earth's surface and direct its realization. The watery landscape of the Venetian Lagoon exemplifies the fourth phase of the realization of paradise on earth, though it is not to be seen in the painting. In fact, it does not need a painting to show it, for it is present all around the visitors as a materialised reality ready to be experienced.

Fortunately, the founders and first builders of Venice were sufficiently sensitive to allow the germination of the seeds of perfection, which we have indicated above as the matrix of paradise. They readied it through the artistry of their city planning, through architecture, painting, music, even the way they managed their politics. It is for us to open our sensors to it all and learn. In Venice, one can learn how it is possible to excite the vibrations of paradisiacal quality through culture.

Exercise 17, to harmonise one's vibrations with those of the true reality

Choose any loveable expression of the living earth, for example, a flower, a nearby tree, rock, or mountain. Choose another one each day. Or answer the call of a particular aspect of your surroundings. You can also listen to your own body, for it is a holographic fragment of nature.

Devote yourself for a few moments to your chosen expression of earthly nature. The condition is that you reach out, with the help of your feelings, beyond the apparent form.

In doing so, you come into harmony with the Being of the true Earth. Remain for a while in that state of harmony.

Now go back to your job. You should give your sister Earth a minute of your attention at least once a day.

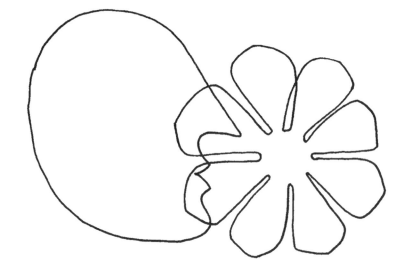

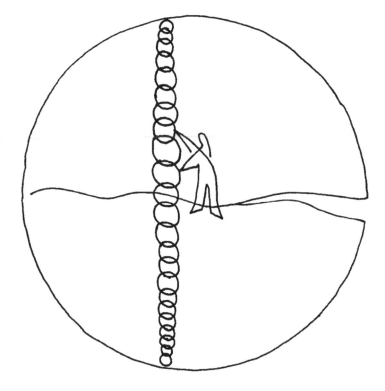

Exercise 18 to experience the matrix of the paradise in the earth's centre

Seek out a place that inspires you.

Imagine that you are throwing a ball of light into the depths of the earth.

The ball rebounds from a firm layer deep in the earth and bounces up high into the heavens.

Gravity causes the ball to fall back into the earth's depths and it bounces up once again off the 'firm' layer.

Go on bouncing the ball of light a few times, down to the depths of earth and up to the heights of heaven and back. The game is now running along your own centre line.

At a given moment, catch the ball in your heart centre and in doing so, try to sense the information that the ball has gathered.

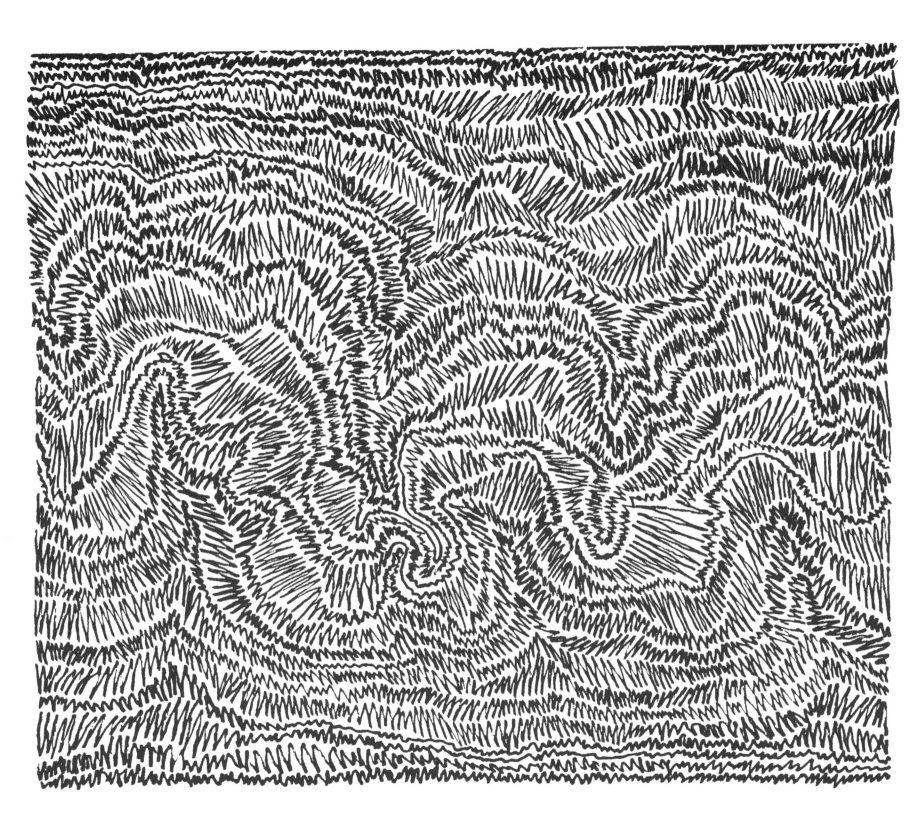

Energetic Drawing 9

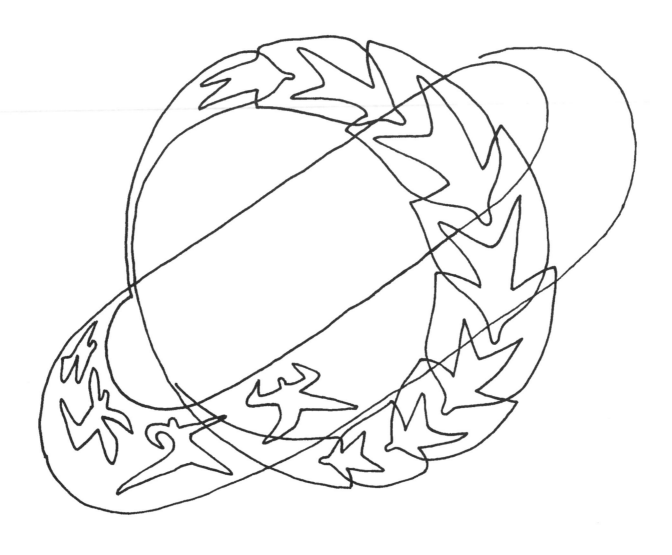

The silent world of souls and, interpenetrating it, the world of incarnate humans.

24.   Presence of the Departed

As long as we ignore the validity of the cycles of rebirth, there are no grounds for talking about any lively sort of relationship with the departed. We do not need to believe any of the versions of reincarnation presented by the old cultures. We need only to open ourselves to the cyclical nature of daily life. Of an evening, when human beings go to sleep, we are dead to the light of consciousness. Seven or eight hours later we are born again to daytime awareness. When evening returns, however, we must 'die' again. The cycle of incarnation is not essentially different. When incarnate, we live for decades. When dead, we may have to wait for centuries for the renewed gift of life in a physical body. Can it be said that we have vanished from life when we are asleep? Can it be said that a person is lost after they are dead?

If we understand space as a multidimensional reality, it is possible for the intellect to imagine parallel spaces for various entities. This tells us that we can be both alive and invisible. The departed live within one particular frequency of space, while we who are alive live within another dimension. What we call 'death' and 'birth' are really two contrary movements through an interdimensional portal that links two different planes of existence. It is however true that in the reincarnation cycle the processes of falling asleep and reawakening are much more complex than in the day-to-day transition. Before and after incarnation the soul carries a kind of light-body. When we are born however, we must collaborate with the natural world to create our body from matter.

So, just as day and night together form a unity, so do the two worlds, in one of which live the souls and in the other the embodied humans. These are the two halves of integrated humankind, each of which is essential to the completion of the other. It is only appearance that suggests that an immense distance exists between the two halves of humankind. We should not imagine that 'the departed' inhabit the clouds, but rather where we living people are busy with each other. It is only a matter of another frequency of existence, and therefore of two world-spaces that interpenetrate each other.

Then why do we not talk with one another, why do we not give each other our support? The people who are not currently incarnate - the souls of the spiritual world, or light-humans - enjoy the gifts of holistic sight. Their insights are not constricted by the barriers of time and space. Because of this they are able to advise incarnate humans where, for example, they should direct their attention and creativity to fulfil the meaning of their lives. We incarnate humans have hands with whose help we can convert ideas and visions into practical deeds. For light-humans this is not possible. It is not only that the two halves of humankind are complementary, they constantly alternate their roles through the cycle of reincarnation.

But what is the use of such a wonderful possibility as mutual support between the two halves of humankind if there is no communication? The task of an interdimensional portal is to enable the dimension of light-humans to communicate with the plane of the material world. The old cultures spoke of communicating with their ancestors. It happens that after their passage into the beyond, most humans are kept busy with their after-death processes. The experiences of the just-completed life cycle need to be stamped in the soul-body's memory. The subtle body needs to be cleansed of the shadows that have settled there through the challenging situations of the past life. While this is happening they are nearly quite unresponsive. However, there are some human souls that are free to devote themselves fully to communicating with the world of the living and assisting their sisters and brothers in times of need. Many of them are entered in the story of humankind as saints and Masters of Eternity, and others one knows intimately from the connections of previous lives. The tumults that our epoch of cosmic transformation are bringing us are scarcely to be mastered without ensuring the assistance of the spiritual world.

25.   The Surprise from the Backspace

We are accustomed to handling everything we do in the space in front of our body. After all, our eyes are so placed that they only see what is before us; we are not like frogs that can watch what is going on behind their backs. Thousands of years ago, the Masters of Eternity tasked the mind to develop a space in which humans could advance their evolution, in the sense of their personal freedom. Because the mind depends on the perceptions of the physical senses to collect its experiences, nearly all its attention was devoted to the visible half of the world.

In consequence, there has arisen a space in which everything important takes place in the light-filled half in front of the body. The mind is not concerned with happenings in the shadowy realm of the backspace. To make a clean sweep as it were, mind has opened a 'miscellaneous file' called the subconscious. Psychologists, sorcerers and students of the esoteric, not students of the mind, are those whose business is in the eccentric backspace. Without arousing any real remark, this has split the ecosphere of earth into two half-spaces. Everything that the present culture deems worthy of attention happens in the light-filled half-space, which meanwhile has become identical with the physical world.

In contrast, the backspace represents the 'dark' half-space. There, everything that the logic of mind cannot digest is stacked up and in part also condemned. Included in this rubbish-tip are the ecosphere's invisible extensions that are part of the foundations of life: vital-energetic phenomena, the elemental consciousness and the spiritual dimensions of space. This one-sidedness can doom our existence on earth. If there is no clear, loving and truthful access to the forces and qualities that are now consigned to the backspace, life will weaken and ultimately be given over to death.

This is the main reason why the self-healing forces of earth have recently been working on the backspace. For humankind, Earth is trying to carry out a thorough cleansing and create a new system in the backspace's parking area. The back's forces and chakra systems will be renewed and set to work… In regard to the landscape, the energy-portals are opened to establish the connection with the inner layers and civilizations of earth's centre. The 'nether world', just like the human subconscious, is newly reorganized and her alienated forces and beings transformed. The halls of the nether world are cleansed. The healing potential and presences of the earth's centre are activated. In summary, this means that we humans are currently living in two alternative worlds. On the one hand, our daily existence is spent in the space of the old consciousness, i.e., in the space in front of our chest. This space is weak and is in the process of passing away. Simultaneously, our ensouled 'I' is challenging us to rediscover our backspace. That space carries the potential to catapult us across the abyss of existential crises. Something similar can be said of the newly forming relationship with the 'nether world'. The inner worlds and civilizations of earth's centre, which represent the backspace of the earth, have the potential to help us beings of the earth overcome the break-up of life systems on the earth's surface. That collapse is now starting. Our challenge is to live in both spaces simultaneously.

If at least a few human beings are consciously living, loving and creating in both halves of space, a peaceful transit through the process of earth transformation will be possible. The 'young' forces, beings, and qualities of the backspace can then flow through the old space in right timing, essentially changing it. Before the life-bearing capabilities of the exhausted world-space are lost, they will be replaced from the supply in the storehouse of the backspace – i.e., from the nether world.

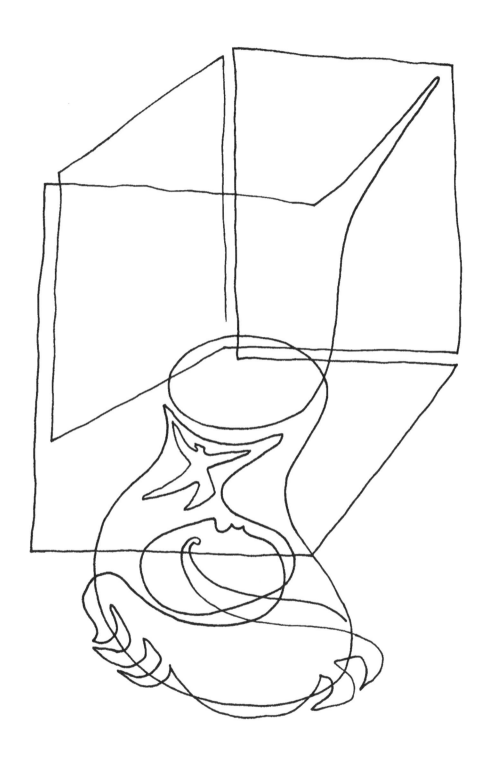

The orthogonal physical space in the 'backspace' of earth's centre.

The workings of the Hallstatt dual pyramid.

Hallstatt is a small place lying in the exact centre of Austria's landscape temple. It could be called Austria's navel and is even visible as such. Rising from the rim of the Dachstein Range is a single pillar-like mountain, 2108 meters high, called the Krippenstein. If one allows one's imagination to enter that mountain's interior, one suddenly finds oneself within a gigantic space that embraces the whole country.

The town of Hallstatt lies on the shores of Lake Hallstatt and an early Celtic culture is named after it, the 'Hallstatt culture'. This came about because at the beginning of the 20th Century hundreds of graves from the early Iron Age were excavated on the high Salzburg plateau above Hallstatt. This necropolis lies along an axis that runs towards a pyramidal mountain that separates the 'valley of the dead' from Salzburg. This 1953 meters high mountain is called Plassen. From its summit one can perceive a 'light city' where dwell human souls not presently incarnate. The Celts obviously wished to bury their departed directly in front of the door leading to their ancestors.

There is yet a third reason for visiting Hallstatt. The Hallstatt landscape is hostess to a wonderful geomantic phenomenon – a dual pyramid of light with a square ground plan. Its sides are roughly ten kilometres long. A dual light-pyramid refers to two pyramids, one of whose summits points to the heavens and the other to the earth's centre. Their base areas are displaced about 90 degrees in relation to each other. The vertical axis that links the tips of both pyramids is centred in the middle of Hallstatt Lake. One usually speaks of such a light-form as a 'merkaba'.

What can be the origin of such a gigantic formation in the landscape? What can its function be? The vertical axis of the composition indicates the relationship between heaven and earth's centre and suggests that it may be an organ of communication between the outer universe and the worlds of earth's centre. If, with the help of one's inner perception, one travels back through the epochs of time, one can ascertain that earth-organs of this nature were established millions of years ago, when earth's surface was still too hostile for humankind to incarnate there. We lived then in light-spaces above the earth's crust. However, the civilizations of that time were already actively preparing the conditions that would allow human beings to live their lives in the physical gardens of earth. To further these preparations, it was necessary to communicate with the soul forces of earth's centre, and also cooperate with the elemental beings of earth's interior. The dual light-pyramids were erected to fulfil this purpose. They are a kind of interdimensional portal.

After human civilization had settled on the earth's surface, their role as interdimensional portals was gradually forgotten and they fell asleep. One could no longer even perceive their existence in the landscape. The current processes of earth transformation have altered the situation. Life on the earth's surface, separated from the sources of Being in both heaven and earth's interior, has become too weak to overcome the present ecological crises. It must immediately resume its vital-energetic, emotional, and spiritual relationships with heaven and the depths of earth.

This is why earth-organs like the dual pyramid at Hallstatt were reawakened and their frozen forces gradually thawed. They are to help life's richness better withstand the shattering movements of the streams of change during the harsh period of earth transformation. Also, dual pyramids of this sort should become midwives to assist the transposition of the old space structure into the newly formed etheric structure of the future earth space.

Exercise 19, to enter into conversation <u>with the spiritual world.</u>

Choose someone whom you love and who has already departed this life and call their presence to your remembrance.

Imagine that you are looking deep into the eyes of the person you have chosen.

As you do so, imagine that the intensity of their gaze causes you to take three steps to your rear, and therefore towards your backspace.

Be aware that in doing so, you are taking the first steps on the road that leads to the hereafter. You may not go any further in that direction or you will lose contact with life in the here and now. On the contrary, make sure you are firmly grounded in the present, because a part of you has stepped over the threshold of eternity.

Simultaneously, open your inner antennae. Sense the breath of eternity. Listen to what the soul you invited has to say to you.

The exercise can also be performed with light-humans whom you have never met personally but who are nonetheless near to your heart.

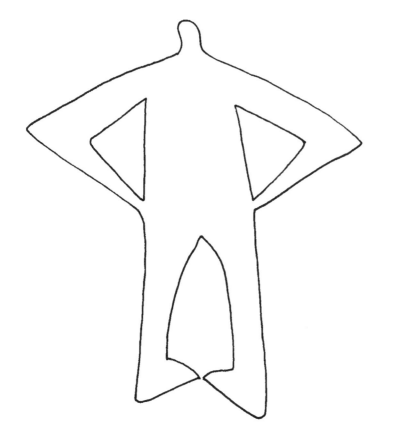

Exercise 20, to experience <u>your relationship with the backspace</u>

While standing, place both feet such that the big toes are touching each other but the heels are spread as widely apart as possible.

In this way, the backspace is opened. Key into the traces of its qualities.

To keep your anterior half-space in balance, you can make a few swimming motions with your hands.

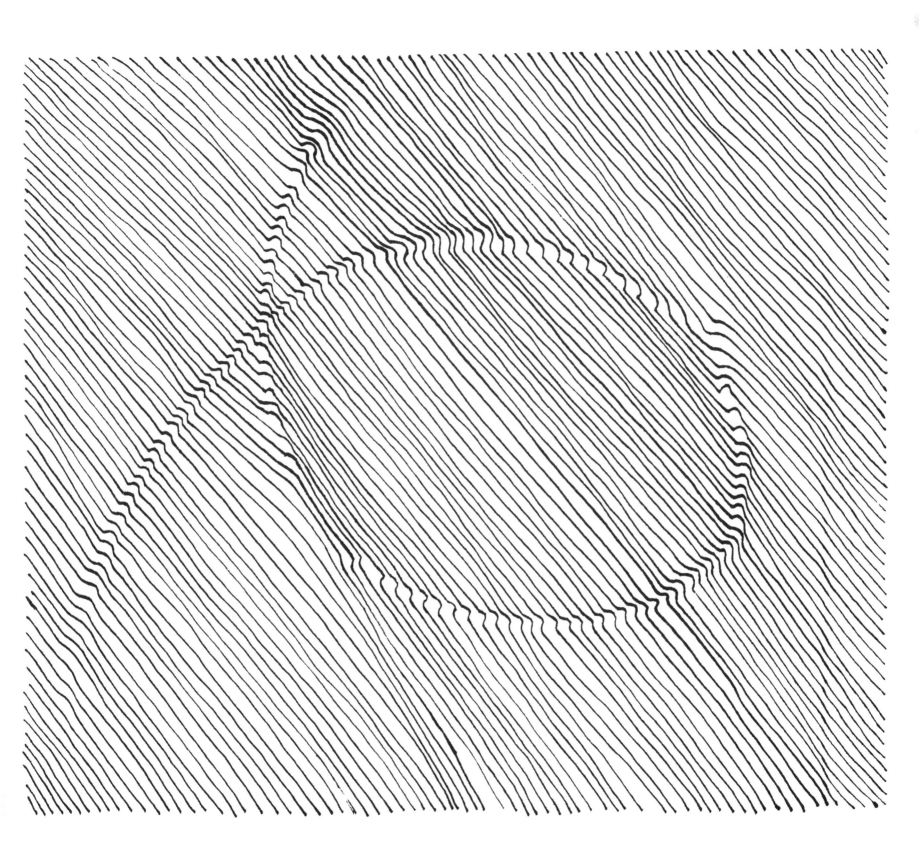

Energetic Drawing 10

82 Cosmograms created by the author and collaborators for the Solar Plexus of Europe Stone Circle, erected in Zagreb in 2005.

27. Universal Language

I wonder how many of us realize that when we humans speak or write to one another, we use a language that only we can comprehend? Did anybody think, when the forms of our present languages were being established, that trees, rivers and angels might express themselves in a type of grammar other than that to which we humans were accustomed? Were they consciously excluded from our circle of communication? Or had the cultures of that time already forgotten that there are other beings of a cosmic and an earthly nature that are also concerned in an expression of the universal consciousness in which they, like us, may want to intercommunicate? The difficulty is that, among ourselves, we humans are accustomed to using the sort of language whose logical syntax enables us to remove ourselves from whatever we are talking about. We are capable of viewing things, beings and worlds from the outside. Our kind of language makes this possible.

The original language is a language of identity. While one is speaking, one is united with the thing or person spoken of. Whoever or whatever is addressed, it is impossible to impede the contact that arises thereby between the two natures, or two hearts. One could call this the 'universal language' for no single viewpoint of the multidimensional universe is excluded beforehand. The universal language is a lively, agile language. Its form is first established in the very instant of being spoken. There exists no previously established structure supported by past arrangements about communication. The universal language represents an open system. The appropriate form of expression is created at the same moment it is first used.

If you want to communicate through the universal language, you are required to listen on all planes simultaneously. The physical form may first be understood when its etheric force field is perceived. The etheric force field may reveal itself when you first become conscious of the symbols encoded therein. Actually, we should be talking of two layers of language. The universal language resembles a colourful multidimensional carpet that is forever being woven: The voice of the Godhead speaks continually, addressing all of life's aspects and beings simultaneously. The voice of the trees weaves its own constant speech. The prayers of our soul incessantly address us. At the same time, human beings are required to deal with concrete matters. We have to agree amongst ourselves what the needs are and how to handle the corresponding transactions. For this purpose we adopt logical speech.

Is it possible to bring both layers of language together? Countless poets and philosophers before us have worked to let the sounds of eternity ring through the linearly structured word. Now an epoch has arisen that desires the reverse from us. The gifts of love and creative power that dwell within human beings should be communicated to other beings of the earth and cosmos. They long for speech with humankind, for we are presently holding in our hands the keys to the fate of planet earth.

A safe passage into the dimensions of the new earth space may well depend on the success of us all joining together in conversation. Consequently there is an intense search for a holographic language. The language of cosmograms is a language of this sort. Specific messages are encoded in the symbols and proportions of the signs we call cosmograms. They should be written down in such a way that they are not only accessible to the logical brain, but also to the consciousness of beings that possess no eyes with which to decipher the shape of the signs. Therefore, it is required that the messages be expressed in the mirror of the corresponding archetypical images, which are clear to all beings. Alternatively, one can make use of the message's reflection in the emotional fields, through which it has access to the sensibility of the heart. A second possibility would be to deepen the physical forms of a sign through the etheric level. Cosmograms are written characters that are alive. Whatever it is that they are telling about, you too are carrying it around in your bosom.

28. New Organs of Perception

Because this modern world is here before us, right under our noses so to speak, it can best be viewed through our eyes. But if we should be more interested in the perception of spherical wholeness, we would need eyes that can see on all sides simultaneously. However, the eyes that we have received as beings of earth, though wonderful, are incapable of perceiving more than the material dimension of reality. Yet we are also interested in experiencing the invisible expanses of earth-space that spread around us. We do not have the eyes for that because, with phenomena of the invisible dimensions of the ecosphere, the deal is that you cannot perceive them if you do not enter into communication with them.

This means that the invisible world remains closed to human beings unless one of us decides to risk an inner relationship with the unknown. This is usually accomplished by making ourselves so wide open to the invisible phenomenon that we allow its qualities to be mirrored on the canvas of our own emotional world. Based on the light-tracks it leaves behind in our emotional world, our consciousness can construct imaginations, i.e., inner images, or receive an intuition concerning the invisible visitation.

Although holistic perception inevitably leads to an exchange with the Beyond, one should not thereby lose one's own 'I'. This is the paradox of total perception, that to gain an experience, one must give oneself unconditionally to what is being perceived, and yet preserve one's own autonomy. Otherwise perceptions become consumed by the patterns and projections attached to the phenomenon that we are contemplating. Our backspace guarantees the best conditions for a perception that excludes this possibility. One could even say that the human back is in the process of developing itself into a complex perceptual organ. There are other reasons for thinking so.

First, if one turns one's attention to an apparition or being of the backspace, one is not disturbed by any physical circumstances.

One is free to contemplate the invisible aspects of the perception without being disturbed by the visible. Second, one can visualise the surface of the back as a membrane that enables the visible aspects of creation, those that are under our nose, to communicate with the invisible, which are 'hidden away' in the shadows of the back. This membrane is especially sensitive to the subtle extensions of reality. Third, there are three pairs of chakras to be found in the back. They are arranged in pairs along the spinal column and it is their precise function to enable the human being to acquire perceptions of the invisible planes of reality.

These six 'eyes at the back' could be called new perceptual organs, for during the epoch of intellect they were sunk in deep sleep. They became unusable. They were first awakened by the reborn interest in the unremarked extensions of Being and are now renewed and ready to take over their role in the perceptual system. The first pair of these 'eyes at the back' is to be found at the edge of the hips, roughly at mid-height. Its task is to perceive phenomena on the vital-energetic plane. When our issue is to perceive the forces of life, then it is this pair that supplies our consciousness with information. The second pair of eyes is tasked with the role of collecting information on the emotional plane of space and then bringing it to our consciousness. The two chakras concerned are positioned on the kidneys. The third pair of chakras is found at the level of the shoulder blades, in the area between the scapulae and the vertebrae. Its task is to supply information regarding the spiritual plane of the surrounding space.

The three eyes at the back ensure that, in every moment, the human being receives a sufficient store of knowledge about the spiritual, emotional and vital-energetic dimensions of the surrounding earth cosmos. Add to these the perceptions of the physical senses, and one is fully equipped to rightly find oneself in the wholeness of life's space.

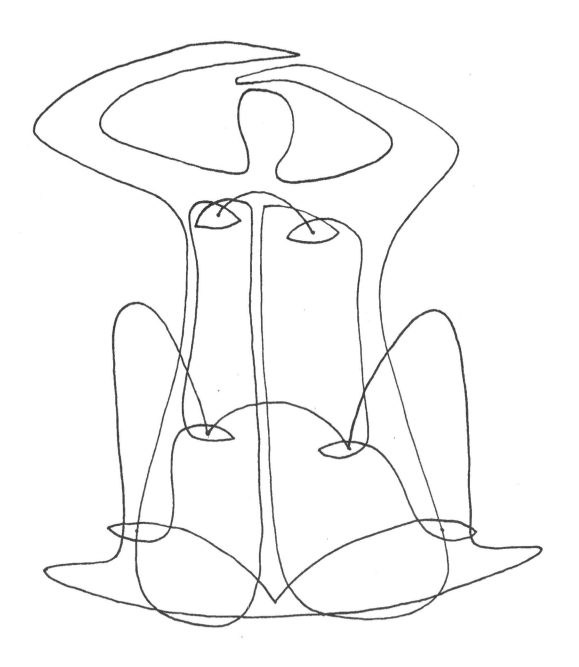

The eyes at the back.

The Cairns of Uggarde Rojr, built of spheres of stone, are able to maintain the exchange between heaven and earth,

so that the landscape of Gotland can receive the vibrations of the cosmic heart.

29. Gotland, Sweden: The Cosmic Heart System

When speaking of the heart system, one should first clarify with which plane one is concerned. On the vital-energetic plane the landscape has three heart centres whose function can be compared to the human heart muscle although there is no physical form attached. They are responsible for constantly flushing out the landscape with fresh life forces. On the other hand, there are heart systems that resemble constellations of stars. They are put together from various earth chakras, which the beating of the cosmic heart – the heart of creation – holds anchored to the earth's surface. It is a kind of resonance system that ensures the working effectiveness of the heart of the universe among the landscapes and wealth of life on earth.

In contrast to the composition of the vital-energetic heart centres, one could speak of the cosmic heart system. The island of Gotland off the Swedish coast belongs to the cosmic heart system of Europe. This spreads out from Gotland across the Teutoburger Forest, the Ruhr District and Brussels towards the Basque region, Brittany and Santiago de Compostella. The island of Gotland lies in the midst of the Baltic Sea as if it were its own continent, washed by the ocean. Gotland's early culture was a Bronze Age one, and its people were obviously at pains to awaken the island's latent relationship with the heart of the cosmos. They have left behind them the Cairns at Uggarde Rojr, located on the island's east coast.

These Cairns are composed of eight gigantic piles of heavy stone spheres. The midmost pile quite closely resembles a pyramid. The other seven also are not cairns in the traditional sense. They were not constructed as a gravesite but rather as a landscape temple. If particular people did happen to be buried beneath them, the goal was to preserve a reliquary. The probable role of the central pyramidal pile was to facilitate the stream of exchange between the inner universe of earth and its outwardly directed complement. The white light of the universe is drawn inward through the 'pyramid' and the black light of earth's centre exhaled to the exterior. The seven smaller cairns ensure that a space can emerge on the plateau of Uggarde through which the pulse beat of the cosmic heart can embody itself on earth.

If one asks the cairns why they were built, they tell of a Bronze Age people who were inspired to erect this composition of stone spheres. These people were moved to it by the Masters of Eternity, to thereby establish earthly resonance with the heart of the universe. Three thousand years later, in the late Middle Ages, a similar mass inspiration moved the simple farmers and merchants of Gotland to build innumerable Gothic churches on the island. Today there are still at least 95 of these wonderful churches remaining. In the middle of each, the figure of the crucified Jesus Christ is displayed as a spring of eternal life.

The Gothic churches of Gotland are scattered over the entire island. They stand as witnesses to a new era of love that Christ's incarnation revealed on earth. These are new impulses of the cosmic heart that could not be rooted on earth through the Cairns of Uggarde, unbelievably strong and sublime though these are. In heaven in the meantime there came an inversion, indeed a somersault, that has transformed the basic frequency and quality of the cosmic heart. Love takes on a personal form. As a result, the simple people of Gotland were inspired to build the 95 wonderful stone-chiselled churches, through which the new frequency of the cosmic heart system could be anchored on earth. This action established the first germ cell in the landscape for the renewal of the heart system of Europe. The new quality of the heart forces was revealed not only by Christ's words at the beginning of our era, for some 1400 years later that same quality was also anchored in the planet's body on Gotland, taking the form of a constellation of sacred buildings, from whence it will be able to gradually permeate the entire heart system of Europe.

Exercise 21, to transform the poisonous forces that pollute our embodied world

Listen for a while to your inner stillness

Ask Mother Earth in the planet's centre to draw to herself your 'grey' powers that poison your relationship with your body and the whole material world, and transform them.

Now you should consciously open the contracted parts of your body (or, if you are working with a place, its corresponding areas) – above all, pay attention to your joints, jaw, sacrum, etc.

Imagine the earth's centre to be a spherical lodestone that draws all your troubles to it, including those that belong to the disastrous heritage of humankind.

Give thanks and rejoice in life.

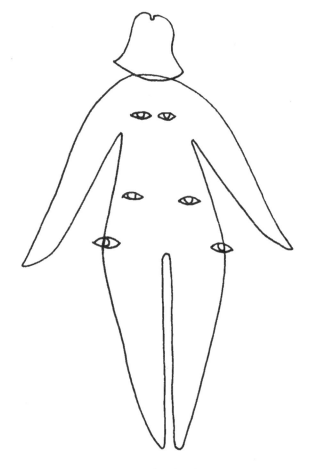

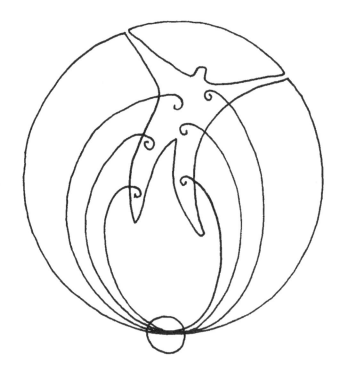

Exercise 22, to perceive the backspace

Turn your back on the place whose depths you wish to perceive.

Be still and without expectations. After a while feelings and impressions will begin to manifest themselves in the area of you back.

Watch the process carefully and make note of any images that crop up in your spirit.

If you want to control the process, use your imagination to press with both thumbs on the following points on your back:

For perception on the vital-energetic plane, press on the edge of the hips.

For perception on the emotional plane, press on the kidneys.

For perception on the spiritual plane, press on the points between the shoulder blades.

When you have pressed the selected pair of points, watch for the impressions that follow immediately afterwards. If necessary, repeat the procedure several times.

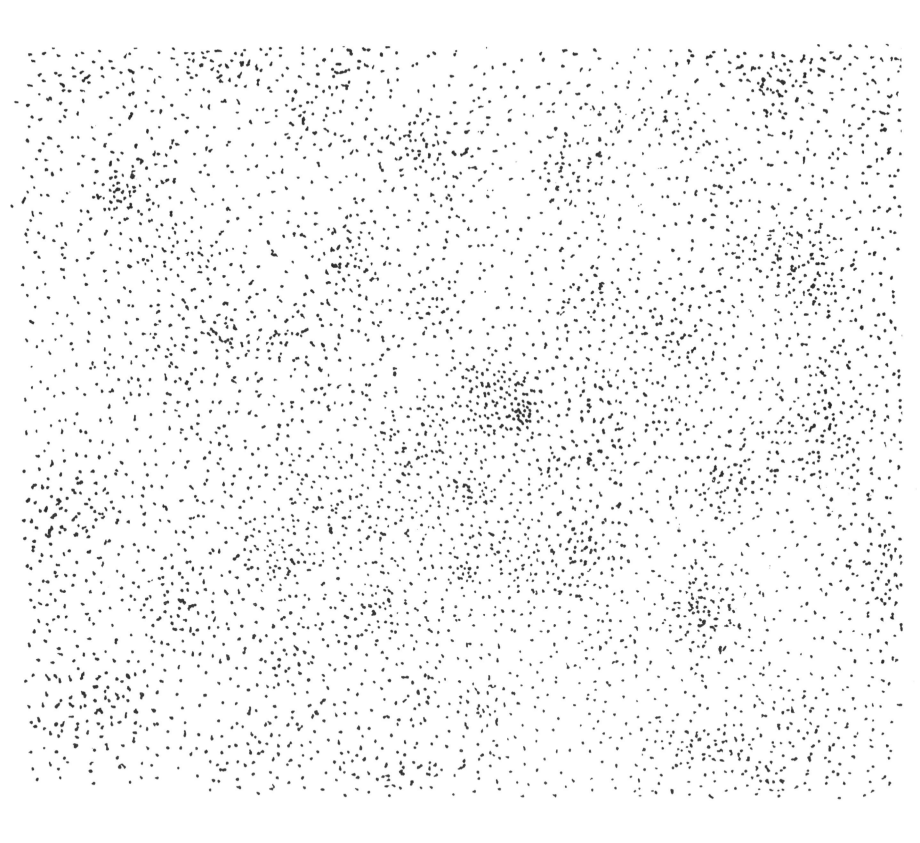

Energetic Drawing 11

The disproportions within the material world are balanced anew.

30.   End of Materialism

Should you believe what intellect has to say about the increasing occurrence of natural catastrophes? Intellect, detached from Wholeness, projects these catastrophes to be the result of the ecological destruction that currently rampages over our planet. Since intellect rules our civilization and for the most part is responsible for this destruction of our natural world, its opinion is not particularly trustworthy. For intellect to criticise itself is welcome and appropriate. However, it raises the question, are we really dealing with true self-criticism or with an artful attempt to conceal the real causes of these upsetting events? It seems suspicious that while so much is lamented, so little is done to stop the destruction of our ecological environment.

We should not close our eyes to the fact that the space we inhabit, and whose collapse we are witnessing, is a creation of an intellect that has made itself independent. We are certainly not living in a natural space. By using the logistical capacities of our own intellect, we humans have created a living space that is too deeply sunk in matter. It reached the point that our intellect could not latch onto the subtle extensions of multidimensional space. They were simply declared to be non-existent. In their place the material dimension of Being was exalted as if only it were real, and was declared to be the dominant reality. Such a fragment, deliberately broken off from the wholeness of reality, is usually called illusion (Maya).

We live in an epoch of cosmic transformation. Do we expect the illusory reality that we inhabit to be spared by the wave of change? The collapse of the four elements, which we can observe happening around us, does not involve the destruction of this wonderful world embodied in matter. The more frequent occurrence of tsunamis, earthquakes, volcanic eruptions and hurricanes do not signify that earth's life force is dwindling. Quite the opposite! We are witnessing the resuscitation of a planet and its natural world, which process is causing the collapse of inappropriate parts of its ecosphere. The exaggerated and forcible materialisation of the natural environment is broken up by apparently cataclysmic events. The same is also true of our material body. New diseases, unknown until now, play a similar role within our own bodies, which are no less a part of the planet's natural world. Involved are processes that certainly may manifest as disease, but are in fact not diseases at all. They appear only because matter is changing. On the one hand the exaggerated materialisation of the nature of the world, as we have known it until now, is dying. It is unable to survive the light of truth. On the other hand the material dimension of Being is being reworked, to be renewed and integrated into the Wholeness. We are speaking of the etherisation of matter, not of dismantling the material nature of the earth's surface.

Because the proportions of the manifested world are changing, all we beings who have a material body are being drawn into the wave of transformation. At this time we are all suffering from the structural alteration of materialised nature. How can we cooperate creatively with this unpleasant process and thereby relieve our pains?

Because matter was wrongly used in the past, the natural openness of the material world became choked with emotional refuse and chained to rigid thought forms. We should first accept the possibility that these 'grey' forces that sit in our consciousness and bones can be transformed. The sphere of the Earth Soul in the planet's centre resembles a giant lodestone. In this epoch of transformation, the lodestone of the Earth Soul is ready to absorb and transform the poisonous forces that burden our incarnate reality. For this to be possible, the germ cells of these forces in our body must open to the liberating attractions of earth's centre. Also, love for creation's bodily form must be rediscovered afresh.

31.   The Politics of the Pure Heart

The concept of politics is often associated with a superficial manipulation of the currents of life in the name of strong individuals and parties that wish to secure their positions of power or material gain. The real meaning of the concept is blatantly different. Since we humans are no longer living in the protected space of tribal communities, we are seeking for ways to live together creatively and happily on a basis of personal freedom – without withdrawing from each other any of life's components.

Because many of life's circumstances concern us not only as individuals but also as participants in a community, we are, as it were, forced to adopt some definite form of politics. In consequence we can say that politics is the art of togetherness. And here we come up against a painful division. Worldwide, more and more people are deciding to devote themselves to essentials. We are no longer ready to bring misfortune down upon our fellow humans and other beings of the earth cosmos. No more weapons, that is the call! Yet simultaneously, our televisions tell of politicians urgently working to kindle the wars they need to drive their colossal economies. Whether the excuse is terrorism or a diplomatic tiff, in every case the consequences militate against the freedom of many individuals and essences that just want to Be; and finally against us too as a holographic fragment of eternity.

Can life really be the way it appears? Or can it be our fractured inner selves that are mirrored in the division described above, whose effects can be observed everywhere on the world scene? It may all begin with the way we relate to each other personally. Am I ready to let my intellect manipulate a relationship because I have difficulty letting go of the usual pattern and giving priority to truth? Am I ready to act positively and even affectionately despite facing an unpleasant challenge? Or would I rather label the provocative forces as an opponent against whom sooner or later there will be war? To make the politics of the pure heart acceptable on the world scene, the first priority is to change the wrongful patterns of dealing with one another by setting an example through one's own actions in one's own environment. Until a sufficiency of fellow humans have decided in favour of a congenial political code of practice, and consequently seek to realize it in every given situation, there is no hope of experiencing it in everyday life.

The next step towards the 'politics of the pure heart' is really challenging. We ask:

Beloved Earth Soul and dear ancestors of humankind! We need your support in our decision to show on the outside, uncorrupted, those things that on the inside we feel to be genuine and in harmony with the cosmic wholeness.

Please create cosmic opportunities worldwide to enable courageous individuals to bring the truth into the open in all possible situations, and so initiate a transformation in the rigidly frozen patterns of political behaviour in the world!

Let such souls incarnate who are wise enough to let the language of their heart ring out in public, despite the fact that the social filter nearly completely prevents such a 'scandalous' outbreak!

To speak the language of the heart in public means accepting the challenges posed by the critical relationships of internal or international politics. One enters the crisis area and acts disinterestedly to help people and landscapes. However, one should not harbour any illusions that the accumulated problems can be effectively solved if the resolution of the crisis leaves the people involved essentially unchanged. Have they relinquished their deadlocked patterns of behaviour? Are they ready to liberate themselves from the dogma of their religions? Have they taken any decisions how they will meet one another in an honourable way and mutually seek for solutions? And, most importantly, are we, who have offered to help, ourselves ready to change? What have we done in our own life that could exemplify for others what we are championing by our political actions?

When the language of the heart rings out in public.

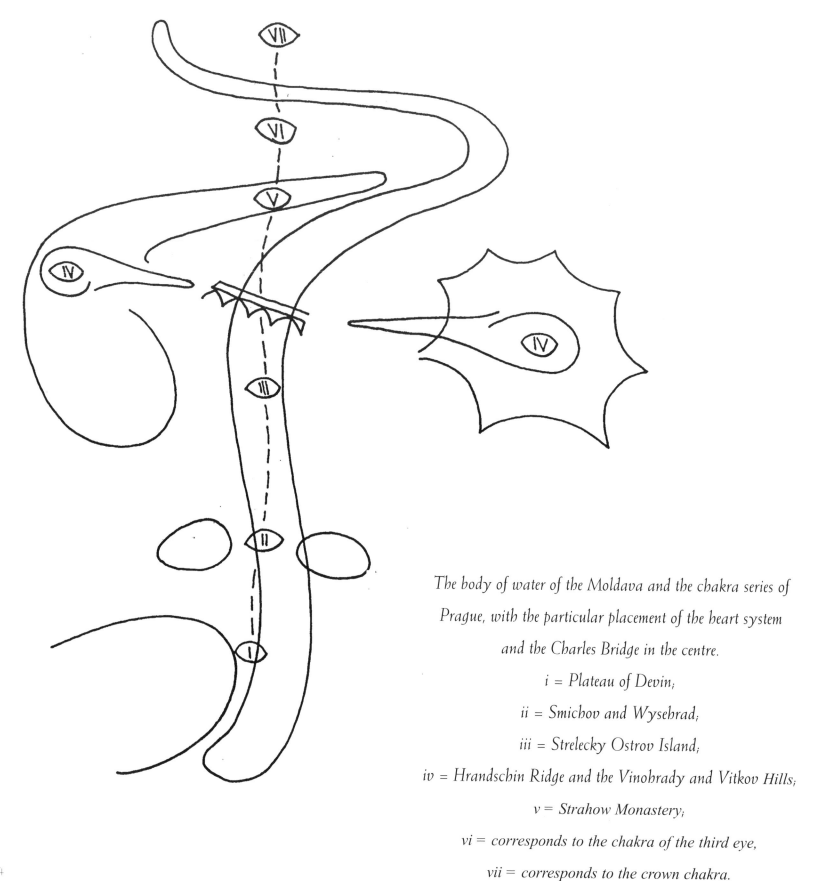

The body of water of the Moldava and the chakra series of
Prague, with the particular placement of the heart system
and the Charles Bridge in the centre.

i = Plateau of Devin;

ii = Smichov and Wysebrad;

iii = Strelecky Ostrov Island;

iv = Hrandschin Ridge and the Vinohrady and Vitkov Hills;

v = Strahow Monastery;

vi = corresponds to the chakra of the third eye,

vii = corresponds to the crown chakra.

32.   Prague, Czech Republic: An Alchemical Landscape

Prague is one of the many cities that lie in the lap of a river. The Moldava River forms a kind of spinal column along which the cityscape has developed. Opening one's senses, one soon detects a series of earth chakras vibrating along this spinal column, and these mirror the chakras along our own spinal column. The landscape of Prague has been settled for millennia and was not only imprinted with the architectural and social patterns of the various peoples but also with its own energetic presence. In consequence, the soul of the Prague landscape was able to develop individual chakras along the river that mirror the vertical sequence of chakras in the human being.

The high plateau of Devin in the south is a storehouse of earth's elemental power and corresponds to the root chakra in humans. Somewhat further north, following the flow of the river, you come to two jutting hills that form an entrance gate giving access to the basin of the cityscape. Wysehrad on the right and Smichov on the left represent the two poles of the sexual chakra. The solar plexus chakra is to be found in the area of Strelecky Ostrov Island. Rising diagonally to the course of the river is the landscape ridge of Hrandschin, which corresponds to the larynx chakra. The castle complex and the Gothic Cathedral of St. Vitus are built upon it. The above two chakras are located in the Stromovka and Troja parks.

And where is Prague's heart centre? One senses that the soul of Prague, moved by the unexpected extent of its heart chakra, intended to give 'the golden town' a special present. An unusually strong heart centre is situated locally, west of the chakra series described above, and underneath the Strahowski Monastery. This heart centre glows like a green sun in the middle of the hill beneath the monastery. However, it does not fit in with Prague's chakra series. To provide the missing complement to the series along the river, a cosmic heart system was developed on the opposite bank of the Moldava. This is a star-like composition of seven power centres that is anchored eastward of the Old City, in the area between the Vinohrady and Vitkov hills. Actually, one should look in the heavens rather than the landscape for the seven power centres. They vibrate high in the atmosphere, but find resonance points on the earth's surface through which to anchor their qualities in the local landscape.

On one of these resonance points, in the Vinohrady area, the Slovenian architect Josef Plecnik has built the church of the Sacred Heart of Jesus. Its form resembles a mighty Noah's Ark. An angelic focus is anchored in its midst. The corresponding point on the Hill of the Holy Cross in Zizkov was recently designated by a lithopuncture stone. The heart centre beneath the Strahowski monastery, nourished by the earth, complements the cosmic heart star maintained by the spiritual world. The power of their mutual attraction gives rise to the alchemical quality of Prague's unique ambience, which combines spirit and emotion.

This uniqueness relates to the power of inner transformation that is capable, during its first phase, of impelling the earthly and cosmic heart systems to creative interaction. During the second phase the consequences of this interaction are coupled with the spectrum of life forces represented by Prague's chakra sequence. We are speaking here of the art of alchemical transformation, through which the germ of life is created, which afterwards is manifested in its full glory in matter. The focus of this multiple interaction is embodied in the celebrated stone bridge that was built for the Emperor Charles IV in the 15th Century. This stands on the axis of Prague's chakra chain and simultaneously lies central between the earthly and the cosmic poles of the heart system. It is no wonder that thousands of visitors swarm incessantly over the bridge. It represents the umbilical cord through which life is nourished during the three-phase process of incarnation, which can be the incarnation of the natural world, or of a human child.

Exercise 23: to experience life's abundance

Settle yourself in the silence.

Imagine that a wonderful flower is beginning to grow upwards from your sexual area.

Its luxuriant leaves unfurl right through your body.

While it is growing up into the heights, mirror-like it unfolds downwards towards the earth's centre.

When the growth process has crossed over the threshold of the larynx, it begins to unfold its glorious blooms in the realm of the head.

Downwards, mirror-like, it develops a concentrated bud, to give you firm anchorage in the earth.

Exercise 24, to vitalise the vertical chakra series

You stand up and start at the root chakra. Your hands form a triangle pointing downwards.

Now you begin to move your hands upward along your vertical axis. The fingertips glide upwards in such fashion that only the backs of your hands touch each other.

At heart level, you quickly flip your hands so that they embrace the heart space together.

As your hands slide further upwards, bring them together in the usual gesture of prayer.

At the level of the third eye raise both hands upward and spread them wide apart, to demonstrate the openness of the crown chakra.

You should perform this holographic gesture a few times, one after the other.

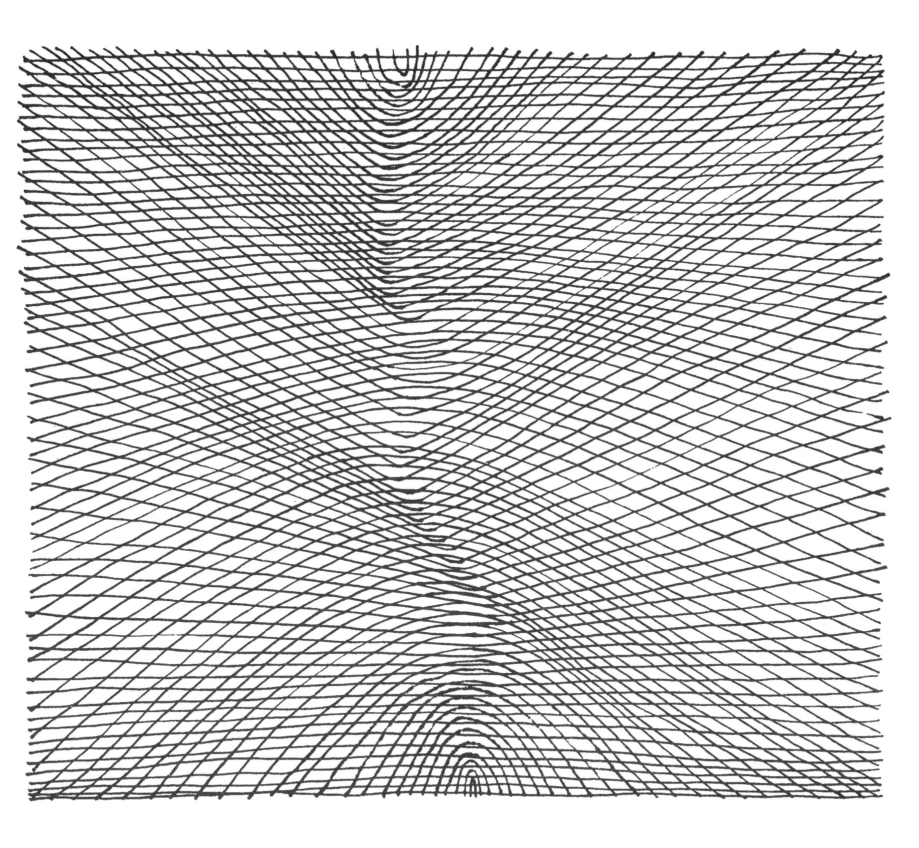

Energetic Drawing 12

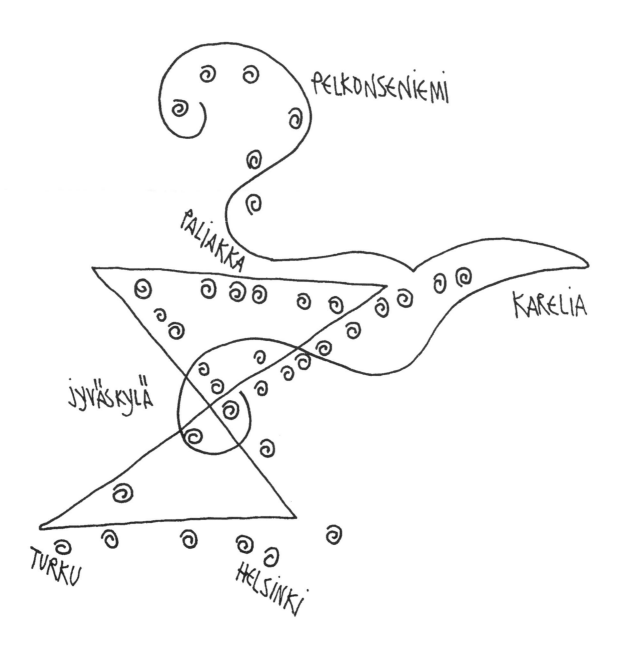

The 36 points of the Paljakka pictogram and the landscape temple of Finland.

Finland: the Country as Organism

One can accept that different places, and indeed different landscapes, have their own power structure. Unless they have a source of power available, they are incapable of sustaining life. This means that places and landscapes should be viewed as entities, every one of which must possess all the vital-energetic organs needed by the life on the earth's surface, i.e., the various kinds of earth chakras, leylines and force fields. In this sense, every place and every landscape is a Holon in itself.

What if a whole country is viewed as a Holon? The Holon of Finland may be interpreted as a perfected organism, thanks to an immemorially old inscription scratched on the sacred rock at Paljakka near Kiuruvesi in the centre of the country. We have here a pictogram of 36 inscribed points that together make up a clearly definable composition: two triangles with apices touching; overall, an hourglass-like composition that appears to be striving upward and runs off in a curve at the top. One can imagine that shamans were able to fly in the spirit above the country and perceive the composition of the most radiant power points of today's Finland. These are the points that we find inscribed in the Paljakka pictogram.

The key to its interpretation can be found if one visits the place in Finland's physical landscape where the points of the pictogram's two triangles touch: this is in the Jyvaskyla region. The local landscape is rich in lakes and islands, and the precise point is on the island of Haikankarki. Centred there is a mighty organ of power whose function is reminiscent of a womb; a column of power descends from the cosmic heights and forms a cupola as it approaches the earth's surface; in the opposite direction a stream of power is rising from the earth's centre; under pressure from the cosmic cupola, the terrestrial forces are pulled apart and distributed outward like stars. Thus a space comes into being where the act of creation is constantly performed anew.

This is the feminine aspect of creation, represented in the pictogram by the above-mentioned line of points that rises upward and runs off in a curve. This curvature is located in Lapland in the Pelkosenniemi area, where it anchors the spiritual aspect of the feminine creative process: its centre is the landscape temple comprising the sacred lake called Pyhajarvi and the Amethyst Mountain. As a process, this should actually be viewed in reverse. It is Lapland in the north that holds the basin where the spiritual essence of the creative act accumulates. Its impulse pours out southwards in a bow to bring the centre of the country into communication with both triangles.

The two triangles, whose apices meet near Jyvaskyla, represent the masculine creative powers. This has to do with the larynx and the ability to form the creative word. The upper triangle represents archetypical forces that are not yet differentiated and know no form. From a human aspect, they can be likened to the forces of the back. We should imagine that the upper triangle glides southward through its central point, and is there essentially transformed. The power of the word – the ability to give form and precise disposition to the creative impulse – is now born within the form of the pictogram's lower triangle. The cities of Turku and Helsinki situated at the base of the lower triangle are today the strongest motivators for bringing the creative word into the open and into physical reality as a formative principle.

Finally, in the Paljakka pictogram, what is the meaning of the 'tail' of three points stretching eastward from the right-hand corner of the upper triangle? That tail represents the relationship with the traditional Finnish landscape of Karelia, which is now part of Russia. It is there that the power-system of Finland described above is grounded.

Exercise 25, to protect
the equilibrium of the earth organism

This exercise is carried out on a body of water. However, one's imagination can also make it work with any watery or ocean surface.

A ball of light is rocking on the watery surface. There is a small child sitting on the ball and, with hands outstretched, is holding it in balance.

If conditions do not favour the child's efforts, one should go to its assistance to help it keep the ball in balance.

The effort that it takes to do this is like the help one has given to maintain the balance of a place, or of the earth as a whole.

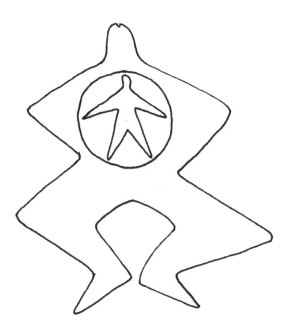

Exercise 26, to complete and protect
one's own Holon, or the Holon of a place

If one wishes to protect and support, either on a continuing basis or in a particular situation, oneself, one's beloved colleagues, one's home, place, country or the earth as a whole, one should use for the purpose the power of the imaginative sphere that is held in one's own inmost heart.

Surround with an egg-shaped, airy sphere of light each of the above-mentioned entities that one has determined to protect and support.

To strengthen the effectiveness of the work, one should slowly turn the sphere while continuing to hold it in one's heart centre.

For this exercise, one should not only visualise what one is doing, but, quite unconditionally, infuse it with the power of feeling too.

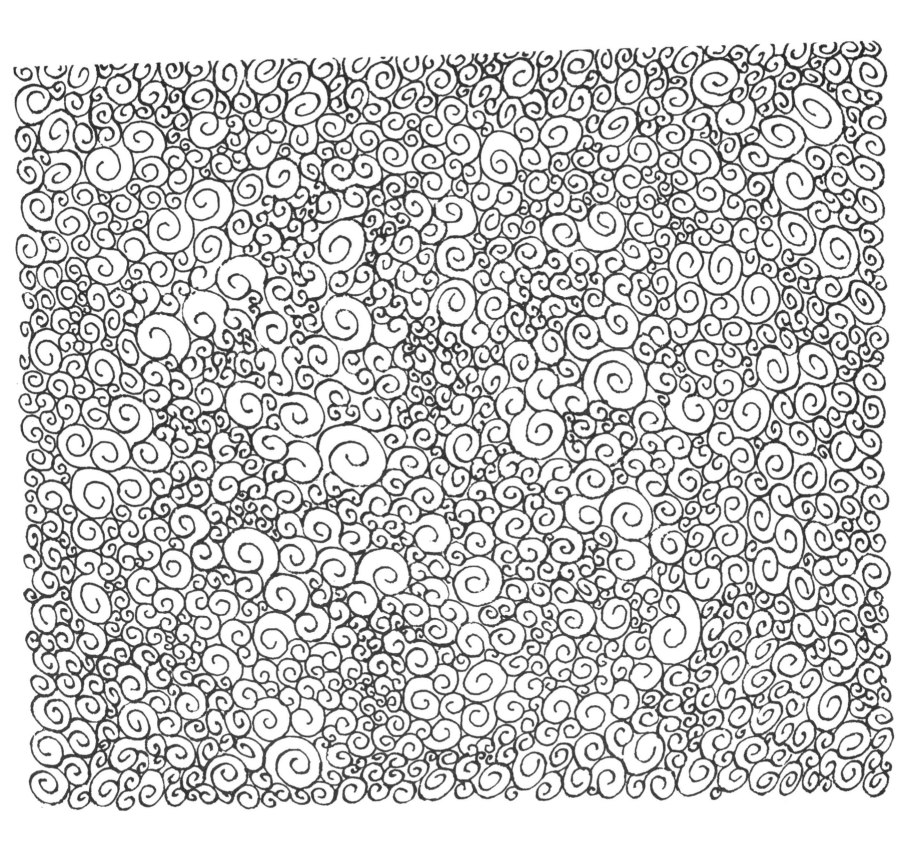

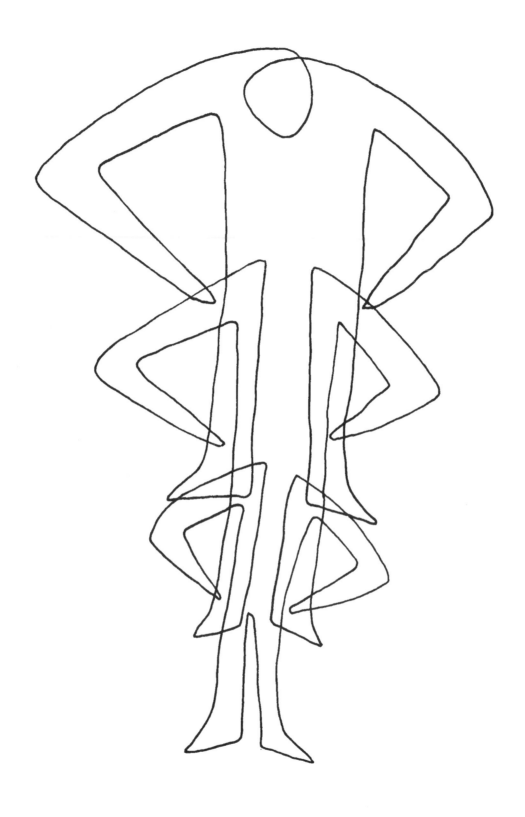

The adrenalin-infused power of Luciferic light.

34.   The Lucerific Syndrome

Though we humans carry quite unbelievable abilities within us, in any given instant the power at our disposal is limited. Otherwise we could inflict far too much damage on our fellows and the life systems of earth. Regrettably this still happens, because we humans have learned to work the switches and divert the course set by the universal wisdom! Since we often feel the power sources that earth has put at our disposal to be inadequate, we have learned to draw the missing forces from other star systems. Using their power, we can give our far-reaching, egocentric projects an artificial shot of adrenalin.

Who has inflicted this on us? When did this begin? These are questions that one does not need to answer. It is a fact that alien forces have been attracted here wholesale. Today they still flow, like a poison, through the veins of human life and the veins of the life processes of earth. This is a potent force that affects the circumstances ruling on the surface of the earth like a narcotic drug. This occurs through the uncannily high frequency of their light. This light is usually called 'Luciferic', because the western tradition equates it with Lucifer, the so-called fallen angel. However, to avoid any negative projections, it should be emphasised that Luciferic light is only poisonous in relation to the frequency of the earth's surface. With the help of this poisonous light, powerful rulers have built their temple complexes, accumulated unbelievable treasure, led their bloody wars of conquest, established lofty cultures and developed mighty religions...

In consequence, a person nowadays can scarcely separate the 'false' light from the juice of life on earth. In any given moment, if a person wants more than is permitted by their bill of life, the stream of Luciferic power is (subliminally) attracted. It immediately manifests what they desire and would otherwise have found impossible to attain. Modern psychology speaks of the 'pact with the devil', by which the persons concerned certainly get what they want, but simultaneously run the danger of losing the core of their being.

Interpreting Earth's wish in this moment of her cosmic transformation, it is to be free of the alien powers so that she may successfully master the approaching cataclysm. She needs a clear head and no drugs! However, she cannot hurl the Luciferic forces back to their home star if we humans are each of us still clinging to that alien power stream.

What can a person do to fulfil the Earth Soul's wish and be free of dependency on Luciferic light? Certainly one could talk about addiction. Self-knowledge is the first key! If one's inward senses are always on the alert to check whether one is following the voice of one's own soul and acting in harmony with the core of one's being, it follows that one is avoiding the danger of attracting the alien cosmic power and so chaining it still more firmly to the earth. In practice this means abstention from wrongful ambitions.

The second key that leads to one's liberation has to do with the development of individual creative power. One is naturally allowed to achieve even exceptional deeds, but only on condition that one's own creative powers, slumbering within us, are awakened. Then you are ready to replace the alien forces. Our goal is not only abstention, but also the development of our full potential.

It is still an open question how we can rightfully honour our obligation to the earth, given that it arose by our bringing the Luciferic powers to earth in the first place. We may do so by thanking the alien consciousness for all the experiences that its power imparted to us. We should also pronounce as follows: 'We are awakened in our own creative power. We do not need you any more. You are free to return to your own star. We are ready to redeem your guilt. Be once again that which you are in your true core being.'

35. The Gift of the Body

The teachings of various religions tell contemporary humans that we have come from heavenly realms to incarnate on earth. In one way, certainly, that may be correct. However, such a vision of the world is problematic because it applies only one lens, using it to declare the heavenly realm beyond the clouds as the true source of our ancestry, and dismissing the body as a mere 'incarnative' tool. In this view, it is the soul that uses the body so it can spend its life on the earth's surface. Using the single lens described above, the body, and therefore the principle of physicality, are declared to be the property of the spirit; and because spirit is superior, it follows that we may use our own body arbitrarily and, finally, also give it short change. However, since our body is part of the embodied earth and natural world, there is a devastating consequence: no clear limits can be set on the exploitation of earth's treasures, or of our companions in the animal and plant worlds. When any such limits are set, it is usually out of fear of personal and collective extinction.

In recent times there has been talk of sustainable development. If we want to ensure that this comes about, it is imperative that we change our accepted mode of perception. And since recently there has also been discussion of body consciousness, it is evident that change is no longer far distant. Recently too, and happily, it has been emphasised that we humans, like animals, plants, lakes and mountains, are natural beings. What does that mean in a spiritual sense?

It means that our source is not only in the heights of heaven, but also in the depths of the earth. In actual fact, we are not born from heaven at all, but from mother earth. To be really precise, the soul is a spiritual form that, through the process of incarnation, surrenders itself to the earth to become born as a physical being. One could compare it to a person going to the showroom and buying a new car. However, there is something essentially different about being born through the earth. One cannot buy one's body. Instead, one has to undergo a fundamental transformation. We are, so to speak, swallowed up by the Earth Soul, to become new born as physical beings. The body with its consciousness and archetypical fundamentals is bestowed on humans so that we can experience the beauty of the terrestrial world; apart from which we also get a brilliant opportunity to grow spiritually through physical experience.

Thus the body is the Earth Soul's living message. Through the process of incarnation the body slowly ascends towards the earth's surface from the planet's cosmic heart, which pulsates in the centre of the earth. In this ascent our 'physical I' passes through different levels of the inward universe of earth until it comes to unite itself with the 'I' of the human soul in the belly of the pregnant mother. Both the 'I' of the human soul and the physical human 'I' are divine entities, equivalent in status. For a certain span of time, they are even united.

The spiritual qualities, energetic structures and physical forms that we inherit from the earth are precisely those entities that desire a soul for themselves, so that they can progress further in their development. This is also true in reverse: the messages and creative thoughts that as souls we bring from the breadth of the universe have the precise qualities that Earth/Gaia needs to advance her creation that is developing on the planet's surface. The exchange is equitable, so we need cherish no fears about our physical existence. Instead, it would be sensible to feel out the energetic and, even more particularly, the archetypical dimensions of our body to better perceive the ongoing communication with its intelligence. Our body's intelligence is a holographic fragment of the Earth Soul, the Goddess Earth. In consequence, we incarnate human beings are a potential expression of her creative will. One can even suspect that Earth has invited us to incarnate repeatedly in her body to help her make paradise real on her surface.

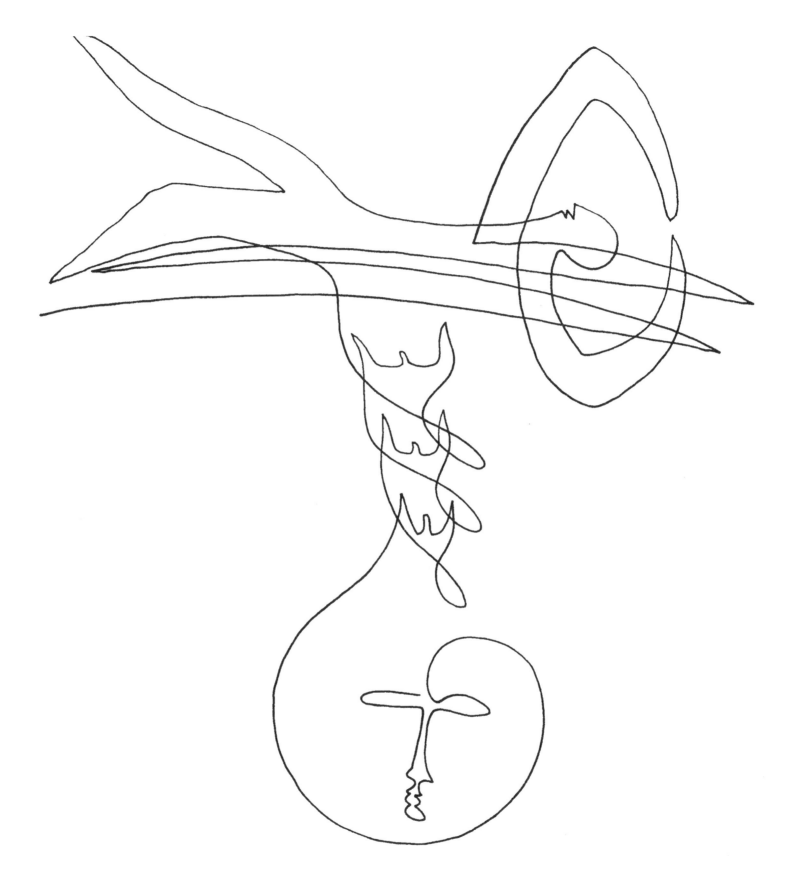

The human body is born on the earth's surface from the archetypical thoughts of the Earth Soul.

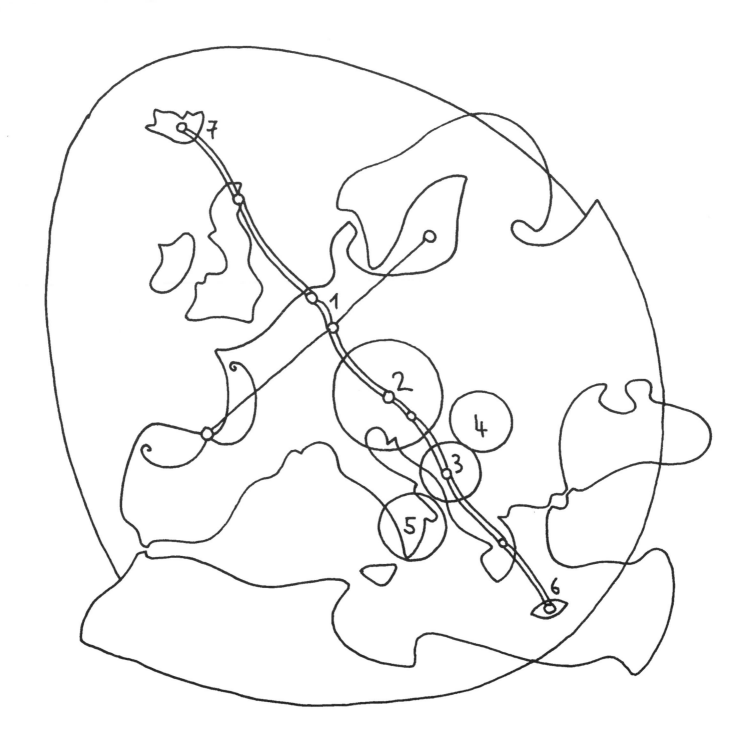

The Holon of Europe with its central 'spinal column'

1 = *the heart system*

2 = *the force field of the solar plexus*

3 = *the Balkans, Holon of the sexual chakra*

4 = *the Hungarian plain, the Yin-field*

5 = *Southern Italy, the Yang-field*

6 = *Crete, the root chakra*

7 = *Iceland, the crown chakra*

36.   Sarajevo, Bosnia: Sexual Chakra of Europe

One can scarcely over emphasise the Balkan situation's decisive importance for the peace of Europe. It is no accident that there have been regular spiritual appearances in Medjugorje, Herzegovina, about 80 kilometres southwest of Sarajevo, ever since 1981. It is the Soul of the Universe that appears there, taking the form of the 'Queen of Peace' and always admonishing people to maintain their inner peace. It is also no accident that, in the middle of a peaceful Europe, the Balkans have seen bloody wars rage through 90 of the past 100 years – that is to say just yesterday.

How does it happen that the Balkans are so decisively significant for the peace of Europe? Let us consider Europe's energetic 'spine' that runs from Crete across the Balkans, Central Europe and Scotland, away towards Iceland. You may see this mirrored in our own chakra series that vibrates along our spinal column, and understand how the role of the Balkans within the organism of Europe corresponds to the function of our sexual chakra.

We are dealing here with the Holon of the Balkans that is centred in Sarajevo and stretches to Belgrade, Kosovo, Sibenik and the Papuk mountain range. To the northeast lies the Holon of the Hungarian plain, remnant of an inland sea. Formerly a giant sheet of water, its Yin quality represents the feminine pole of Europe's sexual chakra. On the other side, southern Italy with its two active volcanoes, Etna and Vesuvius, stands for the Yang pole. The leading Element here is Fire.

The Balkan Holon, lying in the exact centre between the two poles, acts as a point of balance between the Yin and Yang aspects of the sexual chakra. However, since we live in a civilization that does not worry itself about the Yin-Yang balance, the Balkans are forever confronting us with insoluble problems. Furthermore, we have imposed a vehemently masculine civilization on earth, and hence the disturbed balance in the Balkans is mirrored there in retrograde events. The more extreme the refinement and sophistication of the Yang pole – one thinks of high tech culture – the more brutal and primitive is its reflection in the Balkans. Even today, Balkan peace relies on the foreign armies patrolling there. The sole feasible solution is to care forthwith for one's own Yin-Yang balance. In so doing, one must take heed that the fire of one's thoughts is balanced by the water of one's emotions, meaning in practice that our actions should be balanced by contemplation and heartfelt prayer. We should immediately start building a culture that reinforces such qualities. Sarajevo, poised in the eye of a sensitive sexual balance, has suffered most and longest in the recent war. Contrarily, Sarajevo is well known for its traditional religious tolerance. Even during the war the balance between Muslims, Orthodox and Catholics was to some extent maintained.

Sarajevo's role in balancing the Yin-Yang poles is expressed in the landscape by two polarising power centres that stamp their power structure on the cityscape. It is interesting that both centres draw their forces and qualities from the depths of the earth. On the one hand we have a super regional centre that exhales life force from the depths of the earth. It is situated in the 'Energoinvest' area and, energetically, resembles a volcano with Yang characteristics. This is balanced by a power field on both sides of the Miljacka River that vibrates with a more feminine quality underneath the old city; it is a subterranean fairy world there. Between them lies Sarajevo's heart centre (in the Zaltni Dol – Skenderija area), which plays a mediating role between the two poles. All three centres lie along the River Miljacka, which represents a kind of watery spine for Sarajevo. Add that in the east where the river exits from its narrow ravine, the fourth power centre is located – an effusion centre. From thence, the information provided by the constant balancing of the Yin-Yang poles is poured out into the breadth of the surrounding countryside. It would be devastating for the balance of the whole continent if this beacon of light were extinguished. Or has that already happened?

Exercise 27, for deliverance from the alien cosmic forces that are integrated in a person's power system or in the <u>power system of a place</u>.

Anchor yourself in the midst of the radiating beams of your heart. The Luciferic forces belong to the cosmic consciousness and therefore can only be redeemed by the heart's vibrations.

Next, you should decide the context in which you wish to work on the redemption of the alien forces: is it a matter of personal dependency, or the Luciferic forces of a place?

Be conscious of the cosmic sphere that surrounds you. This is where the alien forces can find their home again.

*After this, you should **imagine** that your entire bodily structure is beginning to shake in short, swift movements. You can help yourself imagine this by having your hands make such short, swift movements.*

As you do this, watch how the pulling power of the cosmic sphere draws the alien portion of the light out of your force field. Express your gratitude.

If your concern is with a place, you should imagine that it is the place, not your body, which is shaking.

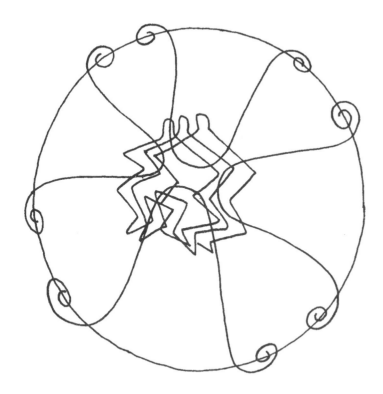

Exercise 28, to experience your own polar opposite

If you are a woman, imagine that a man — your invisible Yang factor — is also living within the same skin as you.

If you are a man, imagine that a woman — your invisible Yin aspect — is also dwelling within the same skin as you.

While you are looking towards your front, your invisible partner is looking backwards, into your backspace.

Accept your polar opposite and remain for a while consciously together.

It can happen that, in your relationship with your inner partner, something needs to change or be discussed. Use the opportunity!

Energetic Drawing 14

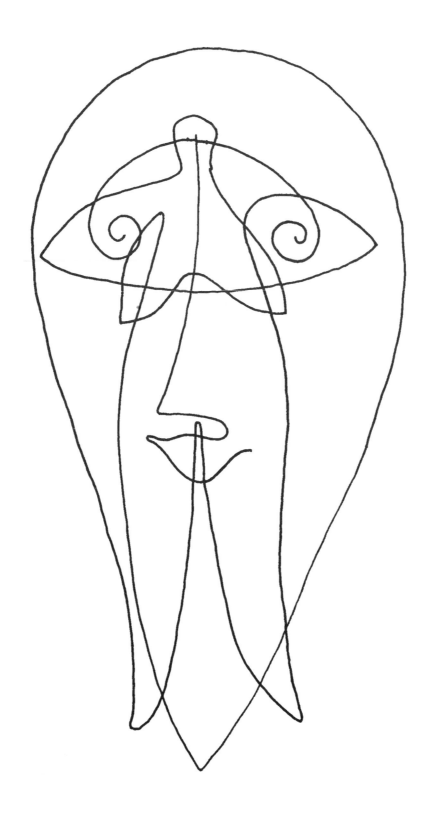

The secret of the Redemptress.

People rave about the Neolithic Goddess. Her figurines, which archaeologists have found on Crete and elsewhere, bear witness to a goddess cult of whose substance we moderners have hardly any concept. Let us imagine Palaeolithic man, how he lived in caves for hundreds of millennia and nourished himself by hunting and gathering the fruits of the earth. The only possibility open to him was to follow the forces of the material world. Is it true then that it was through the Goddess' visitations and teachings that humans learned how to work creatively with matter, make pottery vessels, build villages and a culture? Old legends affirm it. The concept is also supported by the simultaneous emergence of Goddess images in widely different areas.

What meaning does it hold for us today if, in that long-ago epoch, the Goddess appeared as a redemptress to help set a civilization on its feet? Supposing that concept is true, what is happening today to give these putative acts of deliverance a modern relevance? One could say that when human beings reach a point in their evolution where they can go no further but start spinning around on the same spot, then the time is ripe for a revelation. The redeeming impulse hits humankind in an unexpected form. It hurls us around for a while, but then the new evolutionary path is attained. The future stands open before us once again. What was it that helped us on our way? It was the redemptive touch of the eternal soul: an act of divine grace!

Today we are once again part of a civilization that, in respect of evolution, is at a standstill. We turn out more and more goods, but also more and more trash. People clamour for peace but are always starting new wars. It would make the most extraordinary book ever written, how each and every one of us is squatting in a wholly sealed-off mental cage. Where is the redemptress now?

In fact, there is a feminine presence that has appeared to human beings again and again over the last hundred years. She usually speaks through children and pious people who are unable to seal off their mental world so securely as to completely exclude the impulses of the soul. Lourdes, Fatima and Medjugorje are only the most celebrated of the many places worldwide where the so-called Virgin Mary has appeared. As the 'Queen of Peace', she has regularly appeared in Medjugorje, Herzegovina, since the 24th of June 1981. The seers through whom she speaks were then children, and are now grown up. Are the people who crowd on pilgrimages to the sites where the appearances took place aware that they have taken a path that will lead them to meet with their own soul, their innermost 'I'? Are they aware that it is actually their own soul they are seeing and that it must make a wide detour to appear before them in the etheric form of a 'Queen of Peace'?

Because the intellect, detached from the sense of wholeness, has hermetically paved over the inner worlds of modern humankind, the detour is wide and arduous. In the first place, the appearance must arise through foreign children, or as a collective experience, so as not to too much horrify the ego of those targeted. Secondly, the language of the revelation cannot deviate too far from established dogmas and deadlocked portrayals of the world, or people will doubt the credibility of the message. But that is typical of the way of the Goddess. In her soul form, whether of a planet or of a single human, she emerges from the earth's deeps to help humankind free itself from the entanglements we have woven for ourselves.

Revelation emanating from the masculine aspect of the Godhead takes a different form. It is expressed through inspiration and clearly formulated ideas, although usually encoded in symbols. When the Goddess appears, the forms and symbols are not important. It makes no odds to her if her appearance is encompassed by false mental theatrics; it is the emotional touch that is crucial. By touching the soul, she is not only capable of working miracles of healing, but can also change the career path of an individual person, to prepare them inwardly for the coming transformation.

38. The Power of the Original Love

Does anyone even think about the love that streams towards them from places and landscapes? In contrast to love's soft quality, people often harbour rigid preconceptions about whether a person is capable of love, and whether they could not give more. However, the moment that you begin to divide up love's universal wave, its original power is lost. There is no question that you may love landscapes and beautiful trees. But when a person is no longer capable of sensing and reverencing the love radiating towards them from a tree or rock, then love's original power is dead.

There are restrictions on humanity's love: we love and are beloved; we even love God and let him love us. And yet, at the same time trees, rocks, human beings and entire cultures that are not included in the select circle of intimates are all handled lovelessly. Is an example necessary? Think how many people may become enraged, should a person, instead of acknowledging the love of a God, delight in the love of the Goddess in whose essence we bathe.

We are part of a civilization that knows love as a relative force. In fact, in its relationship to anything at all, existent or non-existent, love is thought, felt, and lived. Love can only be love if it is whole, if its vibrations are those of a primal universal power. It is love, not light, that is the archetypical power of the universe; because it is only when love is placed at the beginning of the beginning that one can also participate personally in that beginning. This makes it difficult to push the beginning of creation, the Big Bang, into a far distant past.

It follows that to love means bringing the original creative impulse into present time. It means acknowledging that the universe experiences a renewal in each moment, a healing for every little part of its wholeness, including you and me. People are amazed how it can happen that we, as individual persons and as cultures, are drawn ever deeper into catastrophic circumstances.

People are outraged, for example, at the loveless way that hurricanes treat forests and landscapes. Are we ready to accept that the power of the original love is at work in all this?

Someone, let us say, perhaps the Soul of the Earth or the God of the Universe, is not ready to see a civilization, though a hundredfold divided, lovelessly swept away; and so from the deepest source a wave of love is let loose. In the existing situation on earth, what else can that achieve but chaos and destruction? One can put the same question to oneself, about personal relationships. If one finds the consequences of love to be deeply unsettling or even destructive, it means that one is not ready to accept love as an expression of one's own core of being, which simultaneously represents a holographic fragment of the core of the universe. When love is forgotten or ignored, she becomes terrible.

Does this mean that, without further hesitation, we should start to love and thus save ourselves from the approaching calamities? Regrettably that will not work, because only pure love from the source of love can save. That may be the reason why it is said that to be capable of loving, one should first learn to love oneself. No egocentric love is meant by that. Rather it means that one should free oneself from the fear that rampages around in one's own centre in face of love's archetypical power. It is that fear that prevents one from living out love's original power and making it real. This is a perilous fear because it also threatens to cripple the wholeness of the universe.

To counter this danger and introduce healing, the Earth Soul has for some years been moving an immense throng of elemental powers onto earth's surface. Love's heightened power vibrates in and around us. We are bathed in the rainbow of radiating love. If nonetheless our hearts are obdurate and closed, we will experience no deliverance, but instead an escalation of chaos and misfortune. Fortunately, within this universe there is an aspect of love that is called grace.

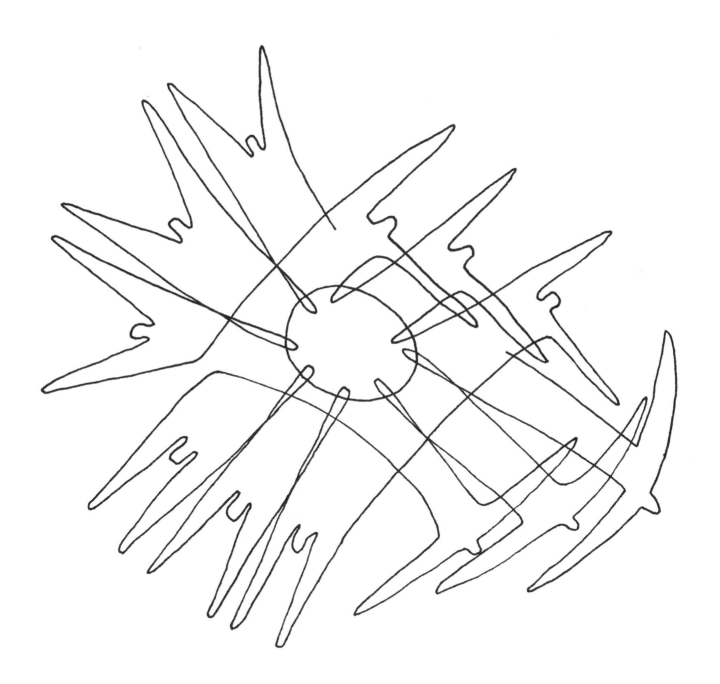

The radiation of an atom of archetypical power.

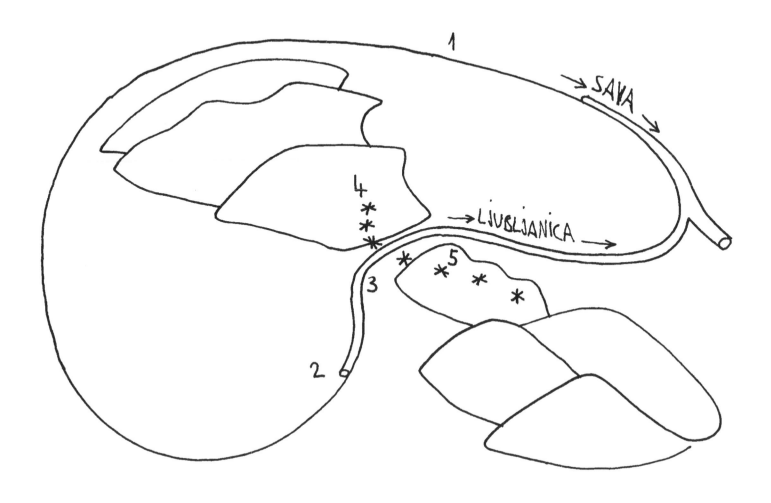

Ljubljana's cityscape and the chain of seven sources of archetypical power.

1 = *Plain of River Sava*

2 = *Ljubljana Fenland*

3 = *River Ljubljanica*

4 = *Roznik Hill with Tivoli Mansion*

5 = *Castle Mount with the City Castle*

39.   Ljubljana, Slovenia: Sources of Archetypal Power

The structure of Ljubljana, capital city of Slovenia, is simple and clearly laid out. Ljubljana lies in a broad basin, whose floor is made up of two plains with distinctly watery characteristics, the Ljubljana-Fenland to the south of town, and the plain of the River Sava to the north. These represent the Yin aspect of the cityscape. The Yang aspect is represented by two hills named Grad and Roznik that lie in the centre of the area where the two Yin expanses communicate through the river Ljubljanica. Both hills are characterised by imposing historical buildings, which underline their Yang role. A mediaeval town castle crowns Grad Hill, and opposite, at the foot of Roznik Hill, stands Tivoli Mansion, formerly a castle. The Ljubljana Yang axis vibrates between both castles. The Yin axis pulsates at right angles to it, between the two plains. The two axes cross each other in the exact centre of the city, just where architect Josef Plecnik has built the celebrated Triple Bridge called 'Tromostovje'.

The city's vital-energetic ground structure could easily be read if we were not in an era of such intensive change. The Earth Soul is trying to break up the blocking structures and introduce healing processes to the earth's surface, and additionally has begun to manifest a new and until now unknown energetic structure: a constellation of archetypical power sources. By 'additional' we mean that the 'old' energetic organism still remains in place. However, its power is bolstered by one of the newly manifested group of power centres – and thereby is also changed. This has activated aspects, till now unknown, of the already existing power centres. When specific power centres are destroyed by our aggressive deeds, substitute centres are created.

To effect change in the old power centres, the constellation of archetypical power sources is organized to be independent of the traditional order. Because of this, the distribution of the new power centres (sources of archetypical power) looks chaotic. They seem as if simply strewn here and there; but, as in the case of Ljubljana, one can nonetheless see that a subtle order rules. Certainly, the city's seven sources of archetypical power do not manifest themselves along the above-described axis system, but, according to one layout, they follow the long axis between the two castles. It would appear that the chain of archetypical power sources stands ready to interact with the Yang axis.

If one follows along the chain, one can learn to know the characteristic centres of the new power system that is now about to manifest worldwide. The first centre on the chain of Ljubljana's archetypical power centres is situated on the above-described Yang axis in the middle of Tivoli Park, below the mansion of the same name. Outwardly, it is a wide avenue, called the Jakopic Promenade. The power centre resembles a light-radiant mandala in the middle of the promenade space. Its task is to instil, in the beings of the earth's surface, the hope that neither the earth itself nor the marvel of life should be lost as earth traverses the current crisis. The second centre is to be found in the burial vault housing the 'Grave of National Heroes', which lies beside the Parliament Building. It acts as a new sort of bonding link between the spiritual world and the plane of manifested being. Next comes the centre located in front of the University Building. This centre supports the interaction between the wide universe and the inner earth. The fourth source of archetypical power is across the river and located on the outside staircase that leads up the Castle Mount along the hill's southern slope. This is a 'point of peace'. Its task is to act as a catalyst, balancing out hostile opposites. The fifth member of the chain lies on the same path but somewhat higher up. This centre causes petrified power patterns and estranged emotional fields in the inner earth to be absorbed, enabling them to experience a transformation. The next centre is to be found on the southern side of Sance, where are ruins of the castle's former outer bailey – and it is a spring of crystal clear healing powers. The seventh centre in the chain is also on the southern side of the castle mount, situated below its third peak called the Orlov Vrh. It is an 'island of light'. Such islands demonstrate the perfection of the seeds of the new earth space.

Exercise 29, to experience the quality of the chain of new forces

First, concentrate on yourself and let the feeling develop that behind your back there is a constellation of beautiful stars radiating brilliant light. The stars stand for forces and beings whose task it is to lend support to personal and planetary change.

In your imagination, let yourself feel light and, rising high above the earth, glide backwards until the constellation is within your body.

What does that feel like, what is going on with you?

Finally, turn back to yourself. The constellation of brilliant stars is once again behind your back. You are grateful for the experience.

Exercise 30: Opening the heart with a prayerful gesture

Put your hands together as in prayer, holding them upright in front of your heart chakra.

When you are ready, begin to slowly open your hands as if you are opening a gate. This is the gesture to open the heart.

When you have made the above gesture and the backs of your hands are resting against your breast and will go no further, you should continue to open the gate in your imagination until it has opened a full 360 degrees.

Now the light of your heart will radiate freely into the world, to bless the life in you and around you.

The exercise ends with the repetition of the prayerful gesture, which serves as a thanksgiving.

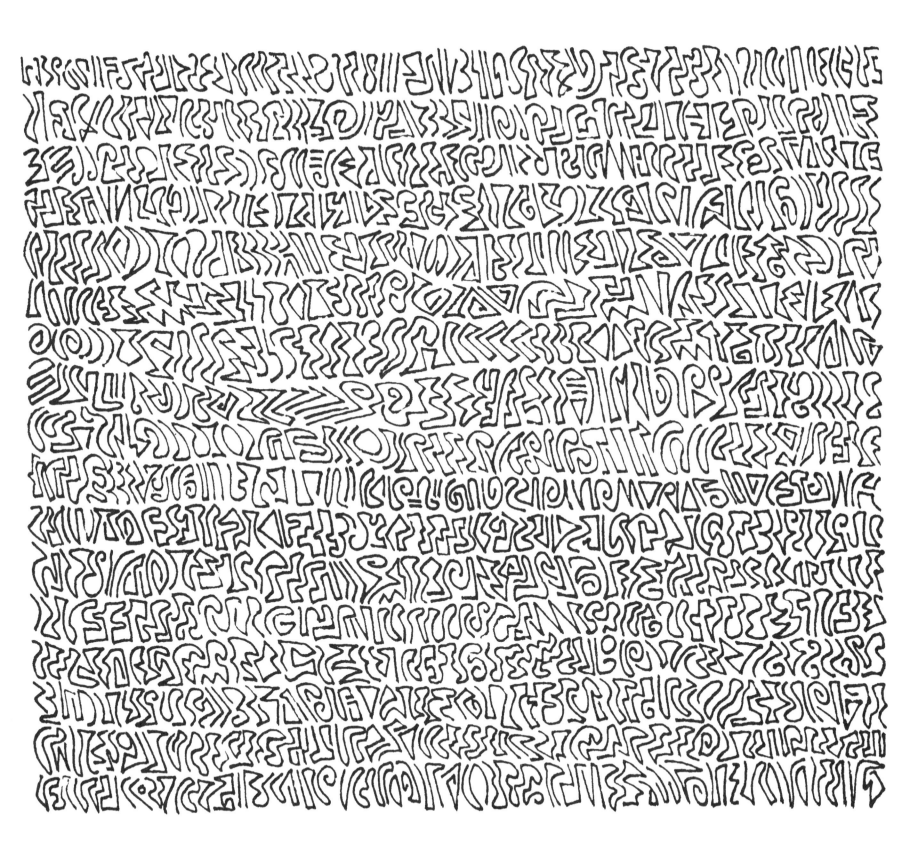

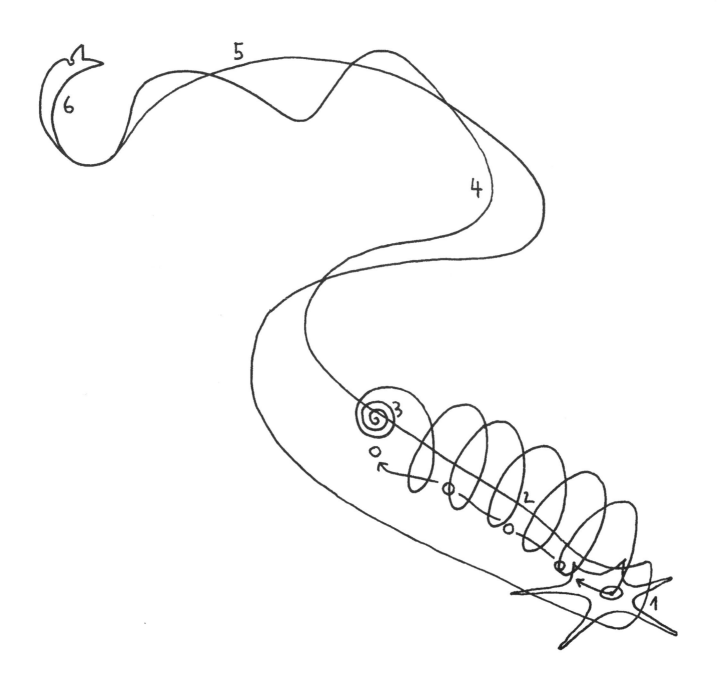

Istanbul sits on the coccyx of Europe's Dragon's Back

1 = *Hagia Sophia and the vital-energetic centre*

2 = *Golden Horn*

3 = *Pierre Lotti and the heart centre*

4 = *Carpathians*

5 = *Alps*

6 = *Pyrenees*

40.   Istanbul: The Dragon's Back of Europe

The vital-energetic structure of Europe can be read in different ways. The ancient myth of the rape of Europa suggests an interesting way to comprehend the wholeness of Europe. The myth tells how the father God Zeus changed himself into a bull in order to kidnap the princess of whom he was enamoured. The princess is called Europa.

If one looks at a map, one can actually recognise the shape of a bull in the outline of the European continent. The Iberian Peninsula represents his head, characteristically lowered and inclining deep towards Africa. The Apennine Peninsula stands for his forelegs, Greece for his testicles. One can imagine Scandinavia to be his tail, held high and turned forwards. The mass of the bull's body stretches out to Asia from whence, according to the myth, Zeus had come to steal Europa. In addition to the physical outline of the continent, one should notice the bull's spinal column: it begins in the Basque country at the back of his skull and proceeds through the whole of Europe in the form of a succession of different mountain chains. It ends in the coccyx, on which the Roman Emperor Constantine built his new metropolis, Constantinople, today's Istanbul. In fact, the mountain chain resembles a dragon's back that holds Europe's force field in a corresponding state of tension.

As stated above, the dragon's back begins at the back of the bull's head in Donostia (San Sebastian) where the Pyrenees climb up from the depths of the Atlantic Ocean. On the southern side of the 'bull's neck' it disappears into the Mediterranean, to rise again renewed from the sea's depths near Nice, this time as the Alps. It attains its highest concentration of force along the main ridge of the Alps. After this it turns into the broad bow of the Carpathians. It finally reaches Istanbul through the Rhodope Mountains, where the accumulated power of the Dragon's Back of Europe is rolled together once again before being handed on to Asia.

Wrong! The power is not handed on to Asia after all. In fact, the role of the coccyx is to block the accumulated power of the mountain chain and send it back, transformed, in the opposite direction. In this way the power of the continent is first consolidated and then magnified. High mountains and mountain chains make an important geomantic system. The pyramidal mountaintops act like antennae to attract the cosmic forces and lead them into the earth's depths. There they mix with the forces rising from the earth's centre. This fusion creates enormous power, which still further strengthens the Dragon's Back of the mountaintop sequence. The plains of the continent are nourished from this heaped-up power.

The function of the rocky coccyx where Istanbul stands is to prevent an efflux of the power of the Dragon's Back of Europe. This mighty stream of power is to be retained, transformed, and sent back towards the Atlantic. To fulfil this demanding role, the 'Golden Horn', where Istanbul is situated, is provided with a special power system. Sitting on the point of the Horn, its beams radiating like the sun, is a mighty vital-energetic centre. This is where the Byzantines built the most beautiful and sublime church in the entire East, the Hagia Sophia. The sun of this vital-energetic centre, coupled with the power of the divine wisdom (Hagia Sophia), seeks to activate the root chakra of the Dragon's Back.

At the opposite end of the Bay of the Golden Horn there is a heart centre that provides some particular help in this regard. The best place from which to track the interaction of the two centres is a lookout point called the Pierre Lotti. The heart centre, situated on the root of the Golden Horn, acts as a mirror that causes the power of the vital-energetic centre (Solar Plexus) on the point of the Horn to rebound with quality enriched. The forces arriving from the Dragon's Back are flung to and fro like a ball between the two centres until they are transformed. After that, they are ready to flow back towards the Atlantic and thereby activate the outflow of the forces of Europe's Dragon's Back.

Exercise 31, for the purification of a space

First, you should decide with which space you intend to work. It can be a house, a landscape or a town. In the last two instances, group input is recommended.

The purification process works with a snowball effect.

Imagine that you are rolling a ball of light through the space with which you are working. All the power structures that have been wrecked and all the emotional garbage adhere to it, so that the ball becomes ever thicker.

Finally, you should bring the ball back to its entry point and bathe it in the power of the colour violet until all the trash is converted and transformed into light.

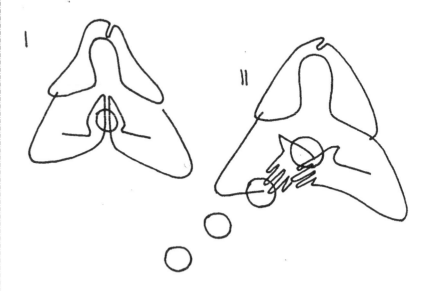

Exercise 32, tear of compassion

If you find yourself confronted by a place, landscape, or being that is suffering, you can change their suffering into joy by giving them a tear of compassion.

Imagine that you are gripping your heart centre with both hands and from it fetch a tear of compassion. Both hands should be used to complete the action, so that it ends with the prayerful gesture.

Now point your hands, folded as in prayer and enclosing the tear of compassion, towards the 'object' of your ritual.

Open your hands and let the tear flow out.

Trace the tear as it flows away, and give thanks.

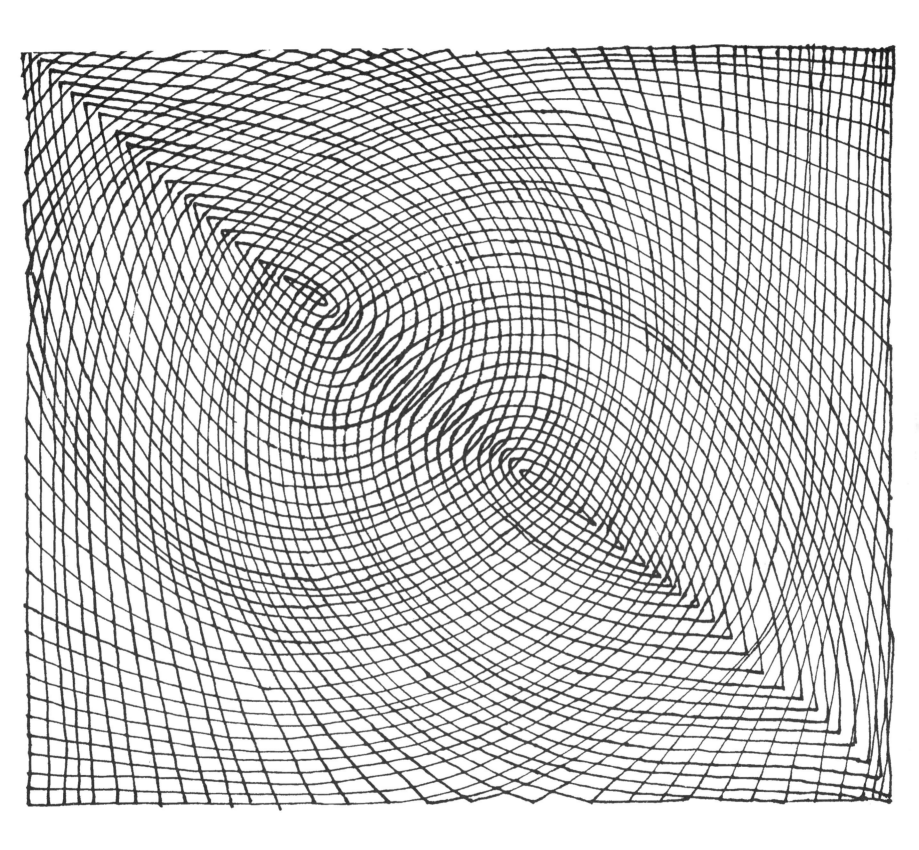

Energetic Drawing 16

Dictatorship of the shadow.

41.   Recycling the 'Dark Powers'

Light and darkness are the two faces of daily life. Nevertheless, a person is shocked when reminded of the 'powers of darkness'. Our concern here is not simply with the forces of the night, but with power and intelligence that has become derailed and lost its duly appointed place in the cosmos. This is an issue to which the ecological movement's ingenious concept of recycling can be applied. This does not belittle the effort to deal with our civilization's unceasing production of garbage, but the problem is not just physical refuse and hidden forms of pollution, like the improvident warming of the atmosphere or atomic radiation. Earth's ecosphere is also burdened by the pollution of its subtle planes, for example, its vital-energetic or emotional dimensions.

The vital forces of landscape spaces are scattered and devalued if used in ways that are not in harmony with the place's essence or energetic structure. Ponderous masses of emotional garbage are hurled into the feelingful atmosphere by exaggerated emotional storms and the poison of fear or mistrust – not only by many individuals but also by entire nations and even religious communities. The idea of recycling beckons us to suggest a means of healing. If a particular force has run off the rails and become destructive, it means that it has lost its role within the universal wholeness. Recycling simply means helping it to return to the circuit of life forces.

The solution is logical and comprehensible, but still faces a problem because the displaced forces have meanwhile acquired a high degree of intelligence. In conscious pursuit of power and profit, humans have too often tried to control and guide these disorderly forces, which egocentrically oriented rituals have impressed with the human will. So it has come about that the powers of darkness have themselves become intelligent and begun to treacherously misuse human beings with the sole object of ensuring their own survival. The human 'powers-that-be' whose will and works abuse and derail the forces of life do not even notice that they are being utilised by the powers of darkness, the so-called 'Archons'.

Finally, one must admit that the 'negative forces' also fulfil a positive purpose. They can mirror human imperfections back to us so that they enter our burgeoning consciousness. If this were not so, human malignity could grow eternally without bumping into any contrary force. At the very moment that one discovers the germ of goodness within something that appears negative, the process of recycling is set in motion. Any human being, who has discovered a personal imperfection in the mirror of their misfortune and then demonstrated a willingness to change, is thereby redeeming the destructive force that previously was forced to embody the corresponding negative aspect. Recycling the forces of darkness begins on the personal plane.

In an epoch of intensive transformation like the present, the Earth Soul's concern is to liberate herself logically from the encumbrance of the derailed forces. She wants to be free of unnecessary burdens in order to act more precisely in everting our space, i.e., turning it inside out. This leads to the new dimension of the Earth Cosmos. In turn, this creates conditions on the earth's surface that bring even the most hidden shadows into the light of day. Human beings are confused. Never before have we been confronted by so many destructive circumstances. We tell ourselves that things will get better, but instead they get worse and worse. This is how the Earth Soul gives an airing to the darkest chambers of our personal and collective subconscious. The 'evil spirits' of the past rise up threateningly, but not however to destroy humankind completely. They are embodied in the many misfortunes of the time in order to achieve the possibility of being recycled. Instead of shying away from their unpleasant presence and continually lamenting it, we should meet their challenge with a smile and cooperate in transforming the powers of darkness.

42. Keys to the New Ethic

Let us imagine the living space that we enjoy in the framework of our earthly universe to be a specific spatial pattern, a specific matrix. If we did not possess the keys to our living space, it would not exist. We would find ourselves in another space. Parents take great pains to furnish their children with the keys to the present earth space. If they are unsuccessful, the children remain suspended in another space, which for us incarnate humans is hard to reach. Often, it is the same space as the one where elemental beings are active.

Something similar happened to earth space as a whole at the beginning of the 21st Century. To avoid the ecological catastrophe towards which our present civilization is steering, Gaia has chosen a new matrix, a new pattern for constituting space. The danger remains that if we do not discover the keys to the new ecosphere in good time, humanity, from a specific moment, may stay suspended in an empty space. We must not only discover the keys, but also use them!

However, it is quite illusory to expect to find these keys in those same realms of consciousness that we are meanwhile able and willing to manipulate. The new holistic consciousness only postulates that, in general, the keys to the new living space can be found. The keys are protected from any kind of manipulation in the best possible way: to be effective, one must put them into practice in one's daily life. These are the keys to the new ethic. They are set out in the form of the seven letters to the seven churches of Asia Minor contained in the First Chapter of the Revelation of St. John. The churches, or more literally, communities, existed in seven ancient cities of which only ruins now remain.

The keys to the new ecosphere are encoded in those self-same letters in such a way that the intellect could not master their message during the past centuries. It appears as if the letters are only concerned with the problems of early Christian communities in Asia Minor. However, they hold subliminal messages that first should be translated into logical speech. Here is one attempt!

Ephesus: Love!

Follow the voice of your heart. In every conceivable situation, ask yourself whether you are really embodying the voice of original love.

Smyrna: Do not fear!

Never try to avoid whatever brings you your personal or collective fate. In every situation preserve your inner peace.

Pergamon: Transform yourself!

Be ready to follow the constant stream of transformation. Ask yourself which of your aspects or activities is calling out to be next in line for change.

Thyatira: Be on the level!

Ask yourself in any given moment whether you are not hiding some aspect of the truth from yourself or others. Constantly explore your heart and spirit to discover whether you have not become the sacrifice to a self-deception.

Sardis: Be whole!

Always be aware feeling-wise of your many-layered wholeness. Keep the great sphere of your being embraced in your consciousness and anchored in your centre.

Philadelphia: Be true to your soul!

Do not forget who you are in the core of your being, and the ideals to which you have inwardly pledged your faith. Remind yourself continually of your spiritual dedication.

Laodicea: Be decisive!

In every situation there are different possibilities to choose from. You are called to make decisions based on the voice of your heart. The only choice not open in this epoch of great transformation is to be undecided.

Possibly it would not be a problem to ignore certain foundation stones of the new ethic if we were to find ourselves together in ordinary earthly life, and not in the vortex of a cosmic transformation.

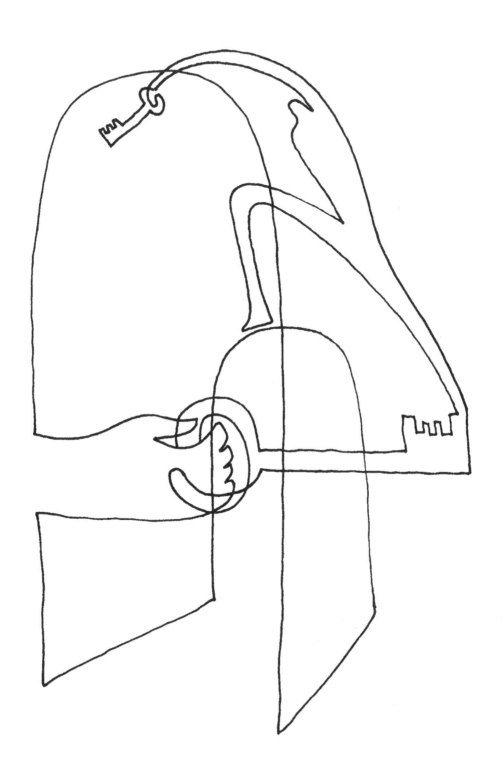

If practiced in daily life, the keys will unlock themselves and the quantum leap will be possible.

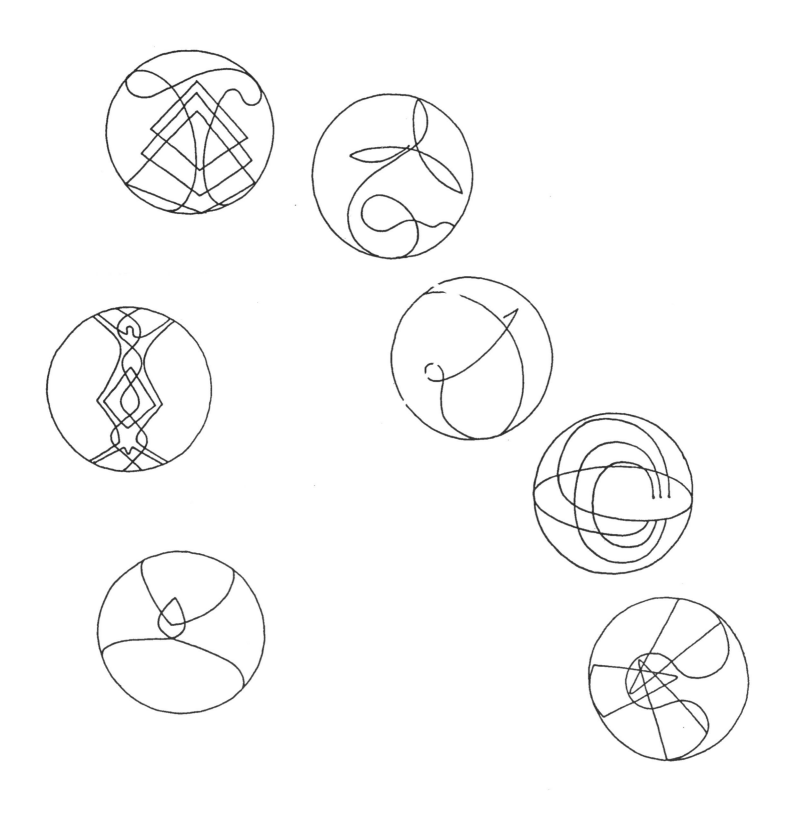

Cosmogram of the seven cities of the Apocalypse, forming a bow from left to right:

Ephesus, Smyrna, Pergamon, Thyatira, Sardis, Philadelphia, Laodicea.

It is quite remarkable that a prophetic writing telling of future events should name wholly concrete places. Ephesus, Smyrna, Pergamon, Thyatira, Sardis, Philadelphia and Laodicea were flourishing cities at the time that St. John wrote down the words of Jesus Christ that have become known as the 'Apocalypse'. They tell of a transformation in earth's ecosystem that then still lay in the future. If indeed this epochal transformation is now in progress, it is incumbent on us to ask why the divine word should have selected these precise cities. Can it be that the issue does not really concern the seven cities that are today in ruins or overbuilt by modern structures, but rather the corresponding places on the earth's surface?

If one looks at these seven places on a map, one sees that they form a sort of bow that encloses a mountainous district about 150 km. in diameter. Lakhmos was the name that ancient geographers gave to that central mountain range. A geomantic investigation reveals that there is a gigantic interdimensional portal in the Lakhmos Mountains. This possibly serves as a model for the way these kinds of geomantic systems appear worldwide. For example, one is reminded of Manhattan, Geneva and Hallstatt.

The portal is made up of four capacious power systems. The first is situated in a very inaccessible district of the Lakhmos Mountains called the 'black hole' where there is an etheric tunnel leading in the direction of the earth's centre. The second system comprises the tunnel entrance, which – pictorially speaking – is encompassed by an oval force field whose diameter varies between 10 and 30 kilometres. The apparent function of the force field is to maintain a level of vibrations adequate to keep the tunnel entrance area free of interference. The third system is a double light pyramid whose plain mission is to guard the relatively autonomous space of the tunnel's structure. The outlines of both pyramids are displaced by about 45 degrees, their apices pointing in opposite directions, one up to the heavens and the other down to the earth's centre. The fourth phenomenon, which plays an important role in support of this whole portal, are the seven places named in the Apocalypse. These shine like a constellation of stars 'above' the portal area and form a kind of portico or vestibule through which to approach the portal entry.

The symbolic language of the seven letters does not designate the portal itself but rather its portico. That is the path that humanity could take at the moment of the great eversion on the plane of the Old Earth, when –according to the vision in the Revelations – our world is turned inside out and the conditions for life extinguished. Then the portal's function would be to guarantee the crossing to the new plane of being where the stream of life flows on. This plane is identified as the 'New Jerusalem'.

The meaning behind the message of the Apocalypse is beyond imagination: the reader's attention is led to the seven keys which will open the interdimensional portal. Not knowing a key, in the decisive instant one is left standing before a closed door. The keys that are now pressed into our hands are the seven foundations of the new ethic. Each is identified with one of the seven places that compose the portico for the interdimensional portal of Asia Minor. The seven places of the Apocalypse represent seven pillars of that portico. This is not just a symbolic representation. Each one of these places possesses a power structure that energetically embodies the corresponding ethical quality. They appear to have been specifically chosen for their power structure to anchor these seven qualities on the earth's surface.

The most important fact is that that the keys of the Apocalypse relate to qualities that every individual human being can embody inwardly and through their life. When the dramatic moment comes, there is no need to travel to Asia Minor in order to access the interdimensional portal. One can make sure of one's entrance ticket right now.

Exercise 33, to work on the
transformation of alienated forces

1. *You are well grounded, centred and surrounded by a protective mantle.*

2. *Decide on what transformation of which of your shadow aspects or derailed forces you want to work. Or you can decide to work on alienated forces that threaten humankind as a whole.*

3. *With the help of the appropriate feelings, experiences or symbols, you should manifest the selected forces along the length of your own back.*

4. *You should simultaneously saturate your entire body and force field with heartfelt love. The power of love should penetrate every cell to enable you to transform even the most negative forces.*

5. *When the pressure of the alienated forces on your back has increased to a dangerous level, you should allow them to glide quite slowly through your body to be changed into pure love.*

6. *Watch the transformation process carefully. If necessary, let still more love flow in.*

7. *Finally, you should experience the radiations and beauty of the force when it appears before you after its transformation. You should distribute it through your personal space as a blessing, or throughout the world if it is a universal force.*

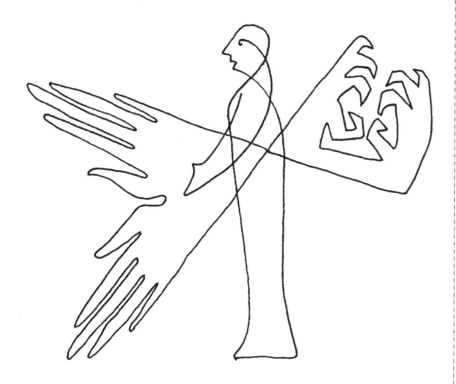

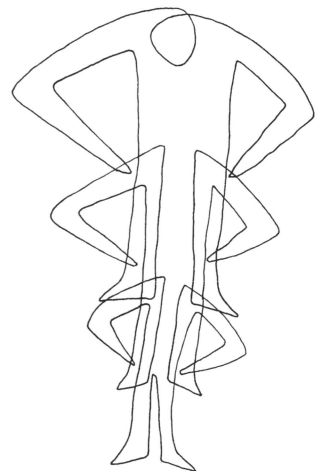

Exercise 34, to connect
with the forces of the four elements

1. *This holographic exercise relates to the chakras of the four elements that are in our body (See my book 'Schule der Geomantie, Thomas Knaur Verlag).*

2. *We begin with the element water. For this we should cross our arms over the breast and then for a little while rub our hands on the places above the breast where the two chakras of the water element are situated.*

3. *After this we go over to the element fire. Rub the earlobes for a while, because that is where the chakras of the fire element are found. This time, do not cross your hands!*

4. *Next in line comes the element earth. The corresponding chakras are to be found below the knee. So you cross your hands and knock on your kneecaps.*

5. *Last we come to the element air. Here we are dealing with the chakras in the middle of the palms of your hands. To activate them, clap your hands once in front of your body and then again behind your back.*

6. *Then, start again from the beginning with the element water, and repeat the exercise at least three times.*

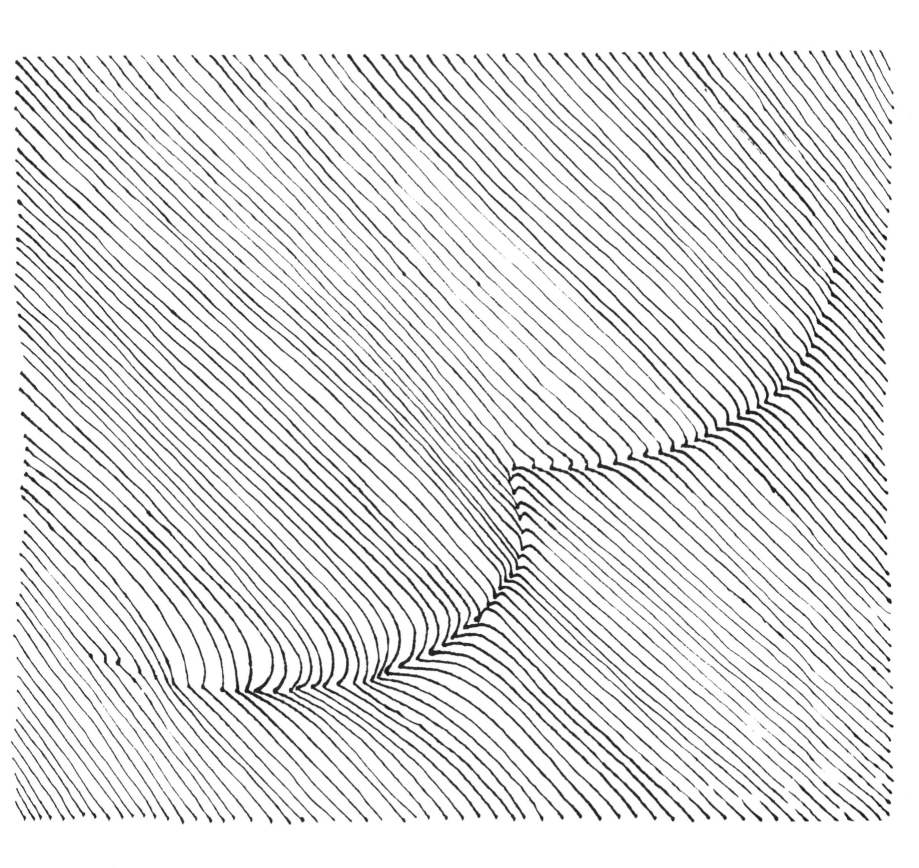

Energetic Drawing 17

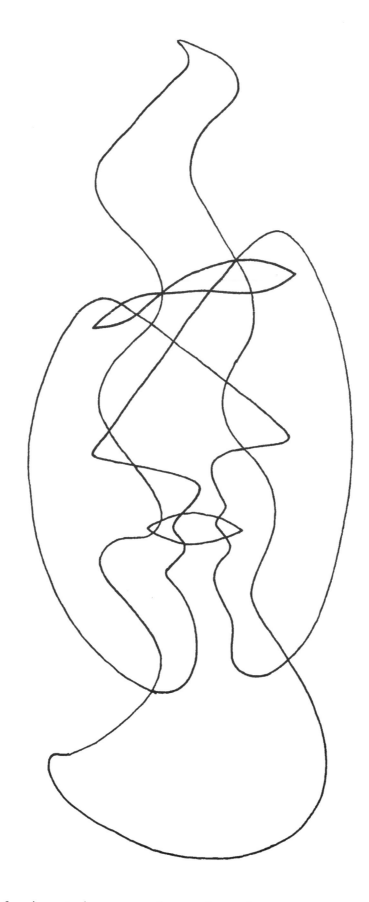

A source of archetypical power simultaneously combines energy and consciousness.

One can understand the whole situation logically without imputing blame. If one accepts the hypothesis that earth is an organism pervaded with life and consciousness, it is logical that she would react intelligently to the danger of the collapse of her life systems. Her reaction can be ranked in two categories. First, she tries to talk, in her own language, with the instigator of the dramatic conditions on her surface. She communicates her message through natural catastrophes and phenomena, for example through apparitions of light, crop circles, etc. Gaia is constantly knocking on the door of human consciousness, which steadfastly believes that it inhabits a mute and silent planet. Second, she intensifies the rate at which her surface receives the forces and qualities to make the necessary changes and reconstruct the wrecked equilibrium. This is a self-healing process employing archetypical forces that otherwise slumber deep in the centre of the earth. New power centres are created – sources of archetypical power that combine earth and cosmos. One could call them 'Chakras of Change'.

So much for the reassuring and logical explanation for which our intellect is thirsting. Contrariwise, reality appears much more chaotic. On the invisible planes there is a violent breakdown of life systems, but this is concealed from the intellect. This effect is the multi-level impact of archetypical forces that in their first phase work destructively. They tackle all aspects of the world's systems, to test which are still viable for the long-term and pure in their being. All the others are gradually drawn into the inner worlds to be transformed. The chakras of change that exercise this unpleasant role may appear demonic to the daytime consciousness. However, in their second phase they exhale cleansed and transformed forces to the exterior. Then, their right name would be 'Chakras of Renewal'.

There are other sources of archetypical power that bring the 'material' for the construction of earth's new multidimensional ecosphere forward into the light of day. In reality, there is no sense of threat in the archetypical sources, but rather a fragrant, paradisiacal quality. There are other chakras of change whose task it is to facilitate communication between the inner earth and the light sphere that surrounds it. This last is a special network of light that has spread itself around the earth to bring into being a kind of womb within which the new earth space can manifest. A fourth phenomenon that can be counted among the chakras of change are the 'light bubbles' or 'light islands' that one finds hovering over the earth's surface. They represent holographic fragments of the archetypical paradise that have risen to the surface from the depths of the earth. Their role is to help accelerate the change processes that lead to the new ecosphere.

The sources of archetypical force newly manifesting in the landscape are so diverse that one cannot really describe them all. Their continually new and unexpected forms of manifestation are overwhelming. A second characteristic of these chakras of change is that they abide by no regular system. They emerge either as freely winding sequences reminiscent of a chain or as constellations that exhibit no logical arrangement. So brilliant is the quality of their light that one could speak of constellations of earthly stars. A further characteristic of the archetypical power sources is that they are twinned with a particular consciousness. One could even say that they appear one day as force and the next as consciousness. Obviously, when considering the archetypical healing forces of Earth, one can no longer separate life force and consciousness. We are looking here at a kind of consciousness that comes close to the consciousness and presence of elemental beings, but is distinct in that it represents a mingling of earthly and cosmic consciousness hitherto unknown. One could say that the sources of archetypical power are simultaneously force phenomena and existential beings.

45.   Return of a Fairy Folk

We humans are so unique, one can but marvel. Travel far and wide in the universe and you will find no comparable living creature. In that context, it is often forgotten that we inhabit a dimension of the universe that was created especially for us and for our parallel evolutions. One should take this as quite normal. The universe is an open system that encompasses sufficient potential space to settle all its evolutions on planes suitable to them. To put it another way, we humans perceive only a particular aspect of the whole and think all others nonexistent. Consequently we find ourselves under an illusion of loneliness that can finally lead us to global suicide. Today it is already obvious that we are incapable of overcoming the accumulating planetary crises without assistance.

The healing forces that work in this epoch of global crisis should remind us constantly that the evolutionary strands parallel to our own are much more significant for our survival than we commonly realize. They see us as a deeply beloved sister evolution and try to tell of their readiness to help us humans in the current situation. As an example, let us take the animal folk. In the course of our long common history, we have given the animals a particular role. Either they were hunted or bred for our nourishment, or for our pleasure. Saddled with such a role and delivered up to us powerless, the animals can give us no help. Rather, we may feel they endanger us. We forget that animals, like us, are cosmic beings. At the very least, the Zodiac in the heavens should remind us of that[2].

Elemental beings are another example. They embody the consciousness of the Earth Soul, which is responsible for the development of plants and nature in general. This involves the soul force of plants and of nature, which we have ignored for the longest time. As a result, plants can no longer provide us with the necessary assistance when unknown and highly dangerous diseases confront us. The third example has regard to a parallel evolution that is completely misjudged. To get a feeling for its reality, you could think back to the aboriginal inhabitants of Europe, the so-called Neanderthals. In the paradigm of modern consciousness they rate as a less evolved race. In fact, the contrary may be true, for this was a race that was more deeply joined to the forces of nature than are we modern humans, the *Homo sapiens*. It is possible that their role on the earth's surface was to embody the elemental consciousness – a particular aspect of fairy consciousness – on the material plane.

The evidence of archaeological digs suggest that both races were settled side by side in the Near East for at least fifty thousand years without having fought each other. The Neanderthals died out 27 millennia ago, at the very same time that humans began to paint their sacred caverns and develop a symbolic language. That was the moment when we humans began to stand on our own feet. Let us take the picture further! Humanity had by then entered an epoch when it was no longer necessary for our evolution to be accompanied by elemental beings on the physical plane. Ancient traditions tell of a fairy folk that long ago withdrew to the invisible plane, and ever since have followed the human story 'from afar'. We have not received any direct help from them since. Now, the global ecological and inter-human crises have abruptly changed the situation. The reins have been taken out of our hands. Quite unconditionally, we need emergency assistance from an evolution that knows the lawful measures and limits of the material plane. And who can provide such help other than our sister evolution who, so many millennia ago, left us to our fate? First, they know the behavioural language that we employ when we exert ourselves on the physical plane. Second, it is this misjudged fairy folk who know the secrets of the transitions we must tread in an epoch of global transformation in order to ensure the further development of life on the earth's surface. How lucky that there are increasing signs of the return of the forgotten fairy folk!

[2] In the German original, the word for Zodiac is 'Tierkreis' = animal circle. (Ed).

Have you ever met anybody like this in your subconscious?

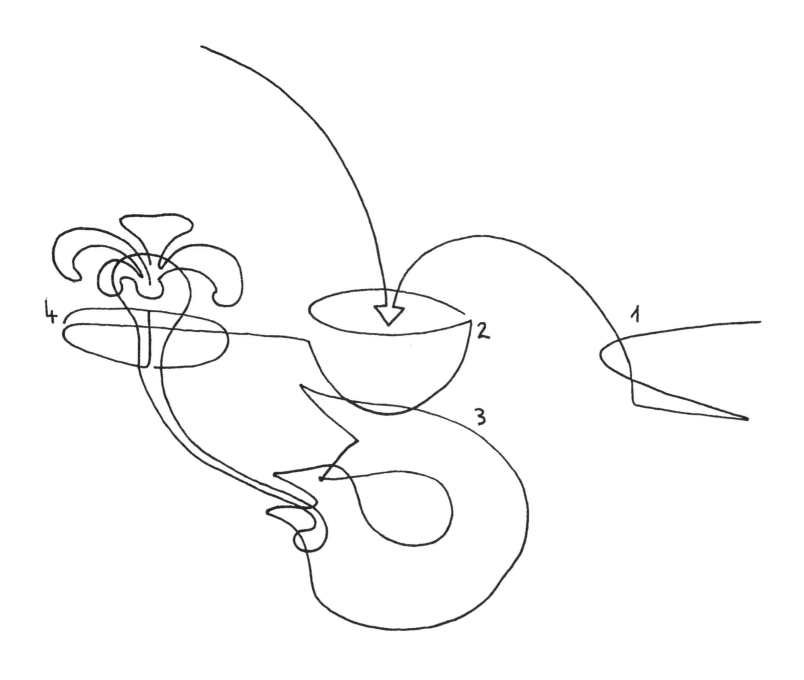

How the permanent tones of Earth's Word come into being at Lake Kinneret

1 = *the Red Sea*

2 = *depression of the Dead Sea*

3 = *Gaia, the Earth Soul*

4 = *Lake Kinneret*

The country that vibrates between the Red Sea and tall Mount Hermon is called 'The Holy Land'. Has Israel/Palestine been given such a label because it mirrors the divine essence of humankind? The so-called Jordan Rift, a deep trough in the earth's surface, can be likened to the spinal column. At one end of this spinal canal lies the Red Sea, which represents the root chakra, and at the other snow-covered Mount Hermon, standing for the crown chakra. Near the Red Sea are two bodies of water that play an important role in relation to the Holy Land's spinal column. The Dead Sea represents the country's solar plexus. The roughly circular Lake Kinneret (which our Bible calls the Sea of Galilee) stands for the larynx chakra. The Dead Sea, lying more than 400 metres below sea level, can absorb a tremendous abundance of life force which it directs towards the earth's centre. Thus the forces of the earth's surface, after their service there and interaction with the cosmic radiation, are anchored anew in the earth's centre. One may say poetically that what the Earth Soul has born, she reincorporates into herself.

And now something extraordinary happens. A portion of those forces that were absorbed are not at peace resting in the lap of the Earth Soul. Having reconnected with 'head office', this part of the terrestrial-cosmic force turns its stream directly around to ascend anew towards the earth's surface. However, it does not hit the surface in the Dead Sea area, but somewhat higher on the Holy Land's spinal column. This stream of terrestrial-cosmic force breaks out onto the earth's surface through the watery membrane of Lake Kinneret. The process can be compared to the functions of phonation and articulation in humans. We breathe the air from our surroundings to sustain our body's life forces. But as we exhale afterwards, we may use a part of the air-flow to produce sounds, or even words. Relating this process to the function of Lake Kinneret means that the lake serves as an organ of planetary speech. This mighty lake has the ability to create sounds and tones that ring through the entire terrestrial sphere. We may ask, is this why the message of Jesus Christ, at its clearest through his words and deeds, was formulated in the area of the lake and then carried throughout the world?

Let us consider the whole process once more. The presence of the Earth Soul, Gaia, vibrates and sparkles within the sphere of the earth's centre. She has available various possible ways to let her word resound among the living beings on her surface. The power centres play a decisive role in this. They can be compared to our larynx chakra, which could be called the organ of Earth's Word. In this connection, we should remember that the larynx is involved not only in the formation of words, but also – in combination with the larynx chakra – in converting the ideas into creative deeds. Analogously, the organs of Earth's Word (earth's larynx chakra) are not just sites that help one to formulate a message and send it out into the world. That is really their secondary function. Primarily, they are creative organs through which Gaia, the Earth Soul, can convert her visions of the wonderful life on the membrane of earth's surface into patterns of creative power. Creative processes are set in motion by means of these power patterns and these are permanently on hand to mould and knead the multifarious forms of living organisms.

The creative word of the Earth Soul sounds unceasingly through the organs of Earth's Word. At Lake Kinneret, the constant tones of Gaia's creative word are carried in a four-stroke rhythm that transits the space of the lake in the shape of a cross. The centres of inhalation at the mouth of the Jordan in the north, and of exhalation at its outflow in the south, represent the vertical axis of the cross. The horizontal axis is formed by the interaction between the lake's Yin and Yang poles. The Nahal Amud ravine in the east stands for the Yin and the En Gev landscape temple on the opposite shore for the Yang pole. In the centre of the lake, where the two axes intersect, there comes an 'explosion of the word'. A sphere of light is constantly forming and simultaneously exploding there, spreading the Word of Earth like a white blossom over the surrounding landscape.

Exercise 35, to gain a deep contact with the natural world

When you take a walk through the countryside, pass through a forest, hike beside a steep cliff or engage in any similar activity, you should find some concrete way to express the love that, as a human being, you feel for the beings of nature.

A tree you can embrace. If the beloved is a mountain, you should let your imagination do the work. Imagine that you are putting your arms around the mountain and pressing it close to your heart. Make the corresponding gestures with your hands.

You should also imagine yourself giving a kiss to rocks, trees and mountains. Imagine that your lips have a long stalk so that they reach the relevant rock, tree or mountain and touch it softly.

In all such cases you should listen for the answer. Look to see what sort of gift the return stream is bringing you.

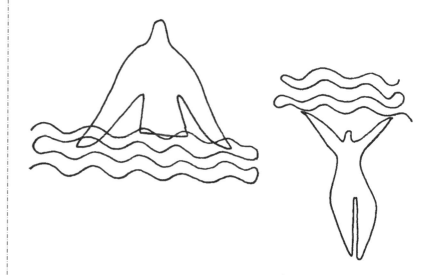

Exercise 36, to experience the quality of the new space

Imagine that you are standing up to your hips in water. Touch the water surface around you a few times.

Now, quickly lift up the mass of water, so that it hovers above your head.

The water is trickling slowly downwards now, like fine drops of rain.

The mixture of air and water produces a frequency corresponding to that of the new space.

You see right through this mixture to perceive the new quality of space.

Energetic Drawing 18

Myth of Romulus and Remus who, in this case, are suckled by a goat and not by a she-wolf.

47.   Animals in Us and All Around Us

If people are hurling abuse at one another, various animal names are often thought to be derogatory. When the animal side of a human being is activated, we immediately think of our darkest shadow aspects. And yet we eat, sleep and have sex not much differently to some animals. How is it then that we are ashamed of our close relationship with the animal world?

In the first place, our intellect has been taught for centuries to regard the animal world as an evolutionary thread that is external to our personal world. In embracing this attitude we scarcely notice that each of us has a fully developed animal inside of us, in the form of a highly sensitive and emotionally gifted organism – our human body. It is true that today many people are turning away from this view. If each one of us is also an animal, we have to question the eating habits that allow us to freely consume our fellow animals.

The decision to nourish the body with healthy food and to follow its rhythms is indeed important. However, all this was decided long ago. The animal within us longs to develop further, but not to improve musculature, rather to develop consciousness. It is interested in communication, and in participating in our creative deeds. The animal in us hankers to live the experiences that we hold jealously under lock and key in the chamber of our intellect. Just consider that our body's intelligence has no access to the thoughts that spin around in our head unless they are consciously translated into the holographic language of feelings and imaginations. The animal in us has no inkling of what we are planning, thinking and creating if we do not put some value on translating all the parallel mental processes into the language of feelings and the body. When life is experienced exclusively as a mental process, as happens now among modern humans, the animal in us becomes desperate. Like a tiger enclosed in the iron cage of our intellectual structures, it sooner or later falls victim to a devastating illness.

Secondly, we should remind ourselves that we are bound to the animal kingdom by karmic obligation. For a long time now animals have been embodying soul qualities in matter, and thereby blazing a trail for us to follow. The more highly evolved animals have even dared to go a step further. Their development of the emotional plane of consciousness has enabled them for the first time ever to create a material expression of the archetype of eternity. Even today, the Zodiac still serves to identify the most important cosmic archetypes[3]. Excavations give evidence of humans having lived among animals for at least a million years: our inner purpose, to learn from them the high art of carrying spiritual impulses over into the forms of the material world. During the last phase of our companionship, their role as domesticated beasts has been of decisive assistance in building our present civilization.

Meanwhile we humans have developed our capacity for independence and creativity to an incredible extent. Now it is time for the pendulum to swing in the other direction. It is the animals that need our care and attention. Instead of exploiting our present superiority by still further refining our ways to control the animal kingdom, we are called upon to help their efforts towards individuation and see them progress. For every human, the simplest and most achievable way to meet this challenge aright is to transform our relationship with the animal within us. To do this, we must learn to communicate with our multidimensional body that belongs simultaneously to the animal and human kingdoms and thereby naturally lends itself as the place for the exchange. To prepare for this, one must first discover the polar opposite to the spirituality that prefers to sit in the head: one could speak here of the grounded spirituality that finds its origin in the wisdom of the Earth Soul. Secondly, one must learn to decode the messages that the animal within us constantly brings to our awareness in the form of bodily sensations, feelings and emotional impulses, and, in natural fashion, incorporate them into our decision-making.

---

[3] In the German original, the word for Zodiac is 'Tierkreis' = animal circle. (Ed).

48. Earth Our Home

If one has not learned to know the wholeness of our earthly home, and also love her, there is no point in tormenting oneself over the devastating consequences of globalisation. One can view globalisation as an outcome of the efforts of many people worldwide to comprehend the earthly cosmos as a unity, and so live in it. But instead of functioning as a global network of mutual support between nations and religious communities, globalisation as currently practiced exploits the cultural and social differences between the peoples of earth to provoke fraudulent increases in the profits of business corporations. To oppose this and further the good side of the developing global civilization, it is insufficient simply to honour the differences between the peoples and religions of earth and forbear from exploiting them, though it is certainly necessary to care for groups and peoples threatened by the maelstrom of globalisation processes. It is also insufficient to turn the earth into a global home for all beings. Even if we made the effort to preserve and revere the nature of all kinds of animals, plants and earth's other beings, still more is needed.

All such efforts would merely be a first step towards making earth our real home. The many initiatives of individuals and groups worldwide have created a general readiness to demonstrate our willingness deal equitably with our home planet and all its beings. However, we can go no further towards making this our global home if we have not decided, once and for all, to abandon our egocentric attitudes and open up communication with the Earth Soul. At this moment, to open up communication with the Earth Soul entails our readiness to raise and discuss the steps she has already taken to safeguard the further development of the planet, and its evolution beyond the expected collapse of its life systems. Let us assume that such a collapse has already happened on the subtle planes of space.

The time difference between the dimensions, coupled with the ring of grace that encompasses the earth, are reasons why we still feel relatively well looked after in the world to which we were accustomed. However, the relationships between religions and culture on the one hand and civilization and nature on the other are becoming ever worse, and this circumstance renders its continuance questionable. To learn which path the earth and her spiritual advisors have chosen to save humankind and the other living creatures from the abyss of death, one must ask the Earth Soul, 'Where do we find the living space that you have prepared, so that we can make our planetary home within it?' But the Earth Soul pulsates in earth's centre far beneath our feet, so how, in general, can we perceive her reply? It can be perceived when a person is ready to accept a particular extension of their being: each of us bears within us a blessed fragment of the Earth Soul, incorporated, one might say, at birth. Through our uniquely self-confident ability to think, feel and make decisions, the essence of the Earth Soul is implanted in each of us in homeopathic quantity. Her privilege of making decisions regarding evolutionary development on the earth's surface will gradually be shared with us humans. To put it more precisely: certain abilities will be activated within us that enable us to serve as creative agents of the Earth Soul. In the paradigm of the present moment, such service means opening doorways for the various evolutionary strands on the earth's surface – including our own – to develop further on a new plane of the Earth Cosmos. On the physical plane, the Earth Soul has no hands available other than our own to construct a bridge to the new dimension of Being; and on her surface, Earth disposes of no intelligence other than the human that would be able to lead the living creatures of the surface safely through the labyrinth of the approaching transformation.

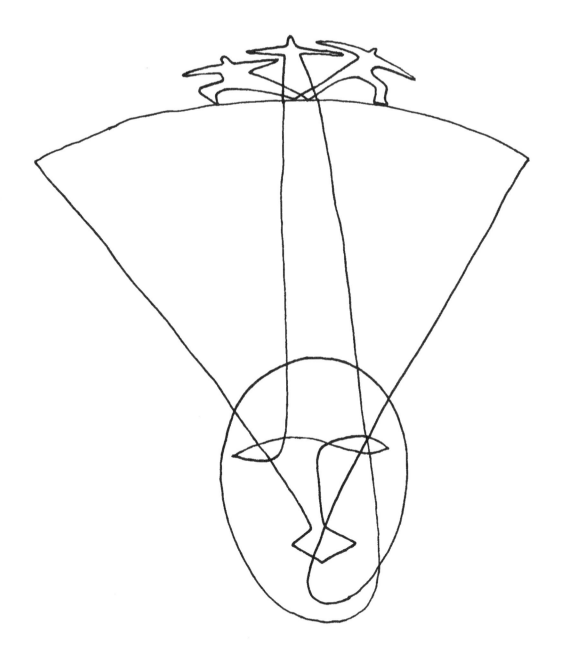

We need to harmonise our actions with the thought-flow of the Earth Soul.

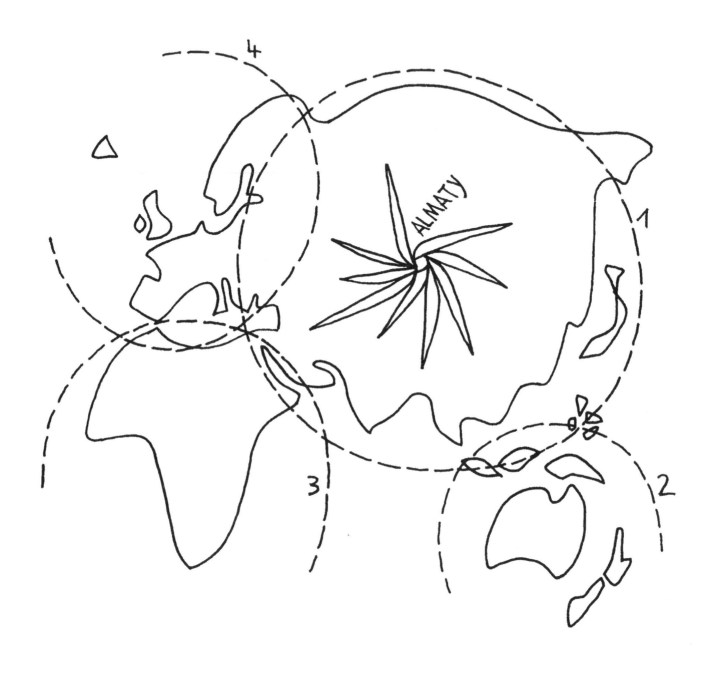

Holon of Asia centred in Almaty.

1 = Holon of Asia; 2 = Holon of Australia; 3 = Holon of Africa; 4 = Holon of Europe

49. Almaty, Kazakhstan: Centre of Asia

If you could imagine yourself standing in Almaty and, with etheric vision, looking across the whole adjacent landmass, you would perceive Asia like a giant rounded space. This is the Holon of Asia. One border can be traced in Bosnia where Islam has slipped deepest into Europe. Part of Finland too belongs to the great round of Asia. There are areas where the Holon of Europe overlaps with that of Asia, as in Bosnia or Hungary. There is also an overlap with the African Holon in areas where Islam is dominant. The eastern part of the Sudan, and Egypt too, can be assigned to the Holon of Asia. In the other direction there are overlaps with the Holon of the Pacific Ocean, for example, in the islands of Japan and the Philippines. One could also pay some attention to the overlap with the Holon of Australia.

If we acknowledge that every continent and every ocean plays a specific role among the units of the planetary body, how should we characterise the role of the Holon of Asia? Let us first consider the others. We may say that Australia is the continent that cares for the relationship with the archetypical forces and images of earth's centre. The oldest species of animals live there, and the bearers of immemorially old human traditions are also still active there today. Europe on the other hand represents the quality of consciousness. The various threads of European philosophy have extensively impressed the thought paths of our global civilization. The Holon of Africa attests to the connection with the planet's vital forces that find their expression through the continent's fiery (Yang) quality. In contrast, the Holon of Oceania embodies Earth's vital forces in their feminine (Yin) aspect.

Interrelating with the above, the role of the Holon of Asia may be to stand for planet earth's creative power. This is the power that is capable of bringing the different qualities of the integrated planetary unity (Holon) into one creative interaction. The feminine-masculine vital forces of Oceania and Africa are interwoven with the archetypical forces of earth (Australia). The synthesis thereby arising is saturated with the power of consciousness (Europe). Now we see Asia's particular role express itself,

enabling the above-described mingling to work creatively among the realms of life on the earth's surface. The Holon of Asia is concerned with a creative power (wisdom) that is capable of entering into the creative processes of matter as well as those of spirit.

Siberia in the northern part of Asia stands for the creative processes that are active in the transformation of matter. India in the south represents the creative processes that have chosen the spiritual plane as their starting point. The ability of the Asian Holon to initiate creative processes is demonstrated in the Holon's exact centre: Almaty, Kazakhstan. A creative planetary chakra, a mighty centre of creative forces, is located south of the town at the foot of the Tian Shan Mountains. The Almaty creative chakra spreads itself over a terrain of 3 kilometres diameter. It is composed of seven giant pillars of light, reaching deep into the earth and high into the heavens. One pillar stands in the middle, the other six are disposed in a circle around it. Their task is to connect heaven and earth and impel the interaction of their creative forces.

The composition of the seven pillars is reminiscent of the wheel of life. In fact, its probable role is to be just such a creative organ, making it possible for the life on earth's surface to develop in all its whole manifold diversity. The task of the central light pillar is to keep the forces of the entire composition of the 'wheel of life' in corresponding balance. The role of the six pillars in the circle is to connect cosmic creative forces with six different creative energies/qualities from the earth's centre. Without these six forces (energies/qualities) there could be no life on the earth's surface. The six forces can be named as follows: interaction between the contrasts of Yin/Yang; fertility impulse; wisdom of the Earth Being; terrestrial time cycles; knowledge of the creative processes; and the love of Mother Earth. Each of these six forces/qualities is brought to the light of day by one of the six pillars, there to enter into a holy marriage with the powers of heaven. If it were not for this, there would be no life to manifest on earth's surface.

Exercise 37, to give the Earth your love

Centre yourself and connect with the cosmic wholeness.

Knead some of the love in your heart centre into a little globule and let it radiate.

Spread the little globule wider till it reaches the edge of your aura. Now let the aura shine with your heart's love.

Spread the aura of love still wider till the entire earth is embraced by the light of your love.

Finally, return to your centre and give thanks for the privilege of being allowed to serve the earth.

Exercise 38, to communicate with the body's intelligence (inspired by the work of William Bloom)

At night, when you lie down, relax your body and stretch out loosely. Fold your hands below your stomach, the fingers pointing up towards the larynx.

Next, take yourself into your heart space. Imagine that you are a tiny man or woman and have come into the heart chamber to gather together as much love as possible. Be honest and responsible, because the body's intelligence cannot be deceived.

Now bring your love down into those parts of the body that have been most neglected. Share it. In so doing, you can visit those parts of your body where difficulties abide.

In this way you can also bring gifts to the forgotten body parts, for example, the most beautiful experiences of the previous day or images of the natural world, not just as pictures, but also as the feelings that accompany them.

Further, after some special experience during the day, you can bring it down into your innermost body immediately. By doing this, you will have brought joy to a faithful fellow wayfarer, who certainly has eyes but can only use them to see when you consciously make it possible.

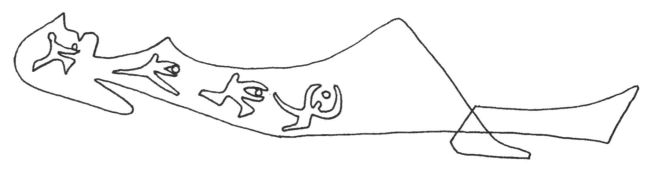

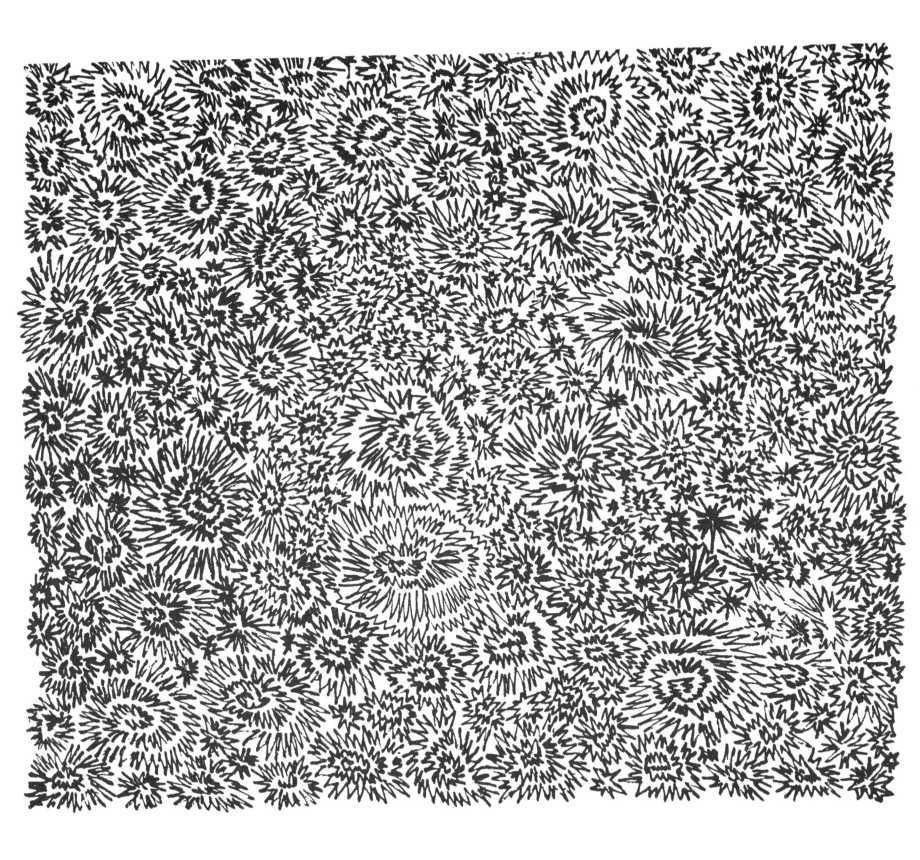

Energetic Drawing 19

Cosmogram of the Philippines: one of the breathing holes of Asia is centred in the midst of the islands.

50.   The Philippines: Breath of the Earth

To breathe is a sign of life. If an organism or a system breathes, it means that it is alive. The earth breathes on all possible planes. An unimaginably large assembly of life force is inhaled in the North Pole (Arctic) area. This is life force that would otherwise permeate the atmosphere but instead is inhaled. One can visualise that these inhaled life forces undergo a process of renewal in the centre of the earth. They experience regeneration. Subsequently the renewed life forces are exhaled in the area of the South Pole (Antarctic) and thence distributed through the whole of earth's atmosphere. This permanent circulation of life force between inhalation in the Arctic and exhalation in the Antarctic is of fundamental significance to the survival of all of earth's ecosphere for the following reason: if every single Holon – every single entity – of the earth is to survive, it must maintain its own respiratory system; based on holographic principles, this means that the stream of planetary breath makes it possible for individual entities on the earth's surface to follow the same breathing rhythm too.

Thus we can see that every place, landscape, and continent has its own respiratory system, just like every human being and every physical living creature. We all breathe in similar fashion. Basically, breathing is an exchange between the life forces that respectively circle through the atmosphere and around us, and the powers that rest in the earth's interior. The forces that circle the earth's surface are saturated with valuable information, which they have amassed through their inclusion in the most varied life processes. Through the same process they have also become laden with cosmic qualities. The living creatures on earth's surface are simultaneously drawing on their power. In contrast, the forces that rest in earth's interior are subjected to a kind of sleep. They find themselves in a phase of resuscitation. There they are neutralized again, which enables them to receive new information, and then, renewed, they are conveyed to the earth's surface.

In principle, a respiratory system consists of two puncture holes that pierce the etheric skin of the earth's surface. Laden with information on life processes and vital forces, an unbroken stream flows through the inhalation hole into earth's interior. In the opposite direction, the life forces, now relaxed and neutralised, flow constantly through the exhalation hole to execute their task on the earth's surface. If the system involves a room, the two breathing holes manifest as tiny power centres. For places like a meadow or a small village they appear as earth chakras of a few meters diameter. If a continental respiratory system is involved, their circumference becomes gigantically large. The huge continental Holon of Asia, which in one direction stretches between Japan and Bosnia and in the other between Siberia and India, has an inhalation hole near its centre, among the Tian Shan range of mountains in the border country between Kazakhstan, Kyrgyzstan and China. Asia's exhalations arise from eight points on the borders of its Holon: in the Philippines; in the area of the Salomon Islands in the Indian Ocean; in southern Sudan; in the Pilis Mountains of Hungary; in the Murmansk area eastward from Finland; in northern and eastern Siberia and in the Kuriles north of Japan.

This means that the life forces in the atmosphere are inhaled in the middle of Asia, and exhaled as regenerated forces through eight landscapes at the edge of the Holon. Afterwards they wind their way through the entire Asian Holon, back to its centre where they are again inhaled. The etheric organism of the Philippines is built around one of these eight giant Asian exhalation holes. According to tradition, it is the island of Panay in the centre of the Philippine archipelago that fulfils this sacred function. The Philippine Islands are arrayed like a necklace of diamonds around this breathing hole in their centre.

Exercise 39, to connect yourself with heaven and earth

As you inhale, imagine that you are sucking your breath from the whole width of the cosmos and sending its stream through your crown chakra onwards to your heart centre.

Pause briefly in your heart centre.

As you exhale, send the stream of your breath down towards the centre of the earth.

Bring your next inhalation up from the depths of earth's interior and direct its stream through your root chakra up to your heart centre.

Pause briefly in your heart centre.

As you are exhaling, direct the stream of your breath upwards to be distributed throughout the width of the cosmos.

Now start again from the beginning and repeat the exercise several times.

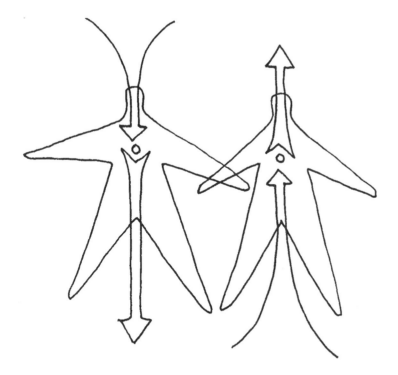

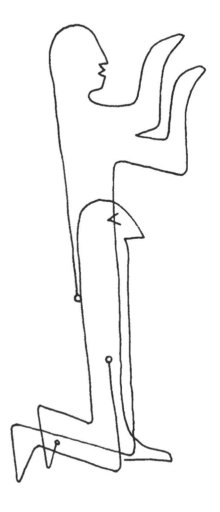

Exercise 40, to sense what are the impulses of earth in a particular place

Put yourself on your knees, but remain kneeling upright.

Be aware that you are now standing on the feet of your soul.

Continue kneeling and, by hearkening to its traces in your innermost being, sense the earth's vibrations.

This exercise can also be used as a perceptual tool to intuit the Presence of a place.

It is also the appropriate attitude for a meditative prayer to attest: 'I am standing on the feet of my soul.'

Energetic Drawing 20

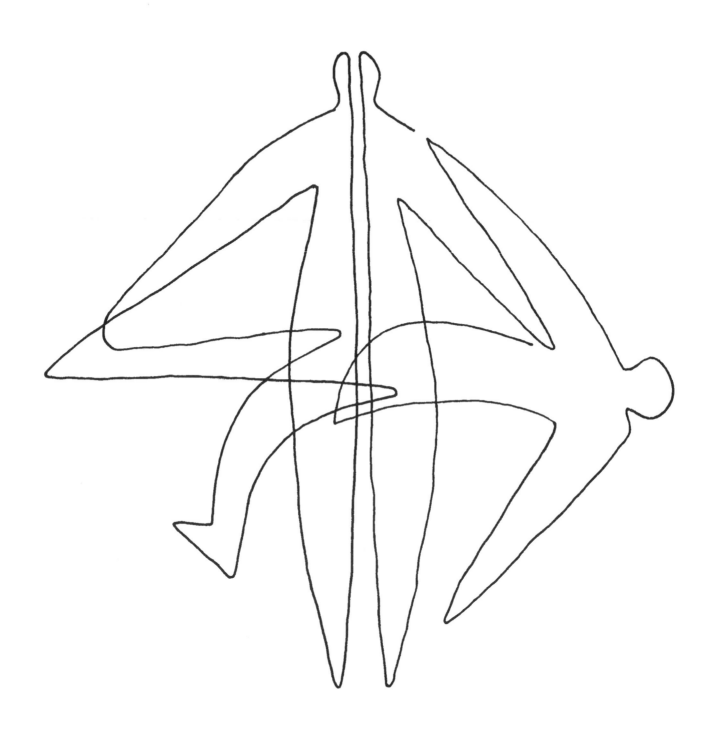

Lay yourself down and experience how the Hara channel
truly represents an alternative connection with heaven and earth.

51.   Sources of the Life Force

If we imagine ourselves standing upright, we can easily visualise how well provided we are with life force. The vertical power channel along our spinal column acts as an energy accelerator. Life forces are sucked in through this channel, either upwards from the earth's centre or downwards from the universe. The sequence of individual power centres (chakras) along the vertical channel ensures that all aspects of our being can share the influx of life forces. However, it would be delusion to imagine that we are constantly nourished by earth and heaven! Human beings carry the necessary forces of earth and heaven within their own Holon, in the storehouse of their aura. We are a holographic fragment of the Earth Cosmos and as such we are endowed from the moment of birth with all that we can ever need in life.

The task of the power channel that runs along our spinal column is, at any given moment, to call forth the life forces as needed from our storehouse, activate (i.e., accelerate) them and place their individual frequencies at the disposal of the corresponding chakra. That is the ideal situation. In the parameters of real life, the storehouses of life force within our aura are often blocked, or even frozen in. For example, anxiety over survival is an unbelievably strong obstructive force that prevents life's abundance from manifesting in a person's living conditions, or even in those of an entire nation. Forgetfulness of one's own centre also leads to a blocking of the sources of the life force, to say nothing of the inhibiting effects of aggressive behaviour. Extend this knowledge to the great Holon of planetary space and one can easily understand how the planet earth, despite her unbelievable reserve of energy, must fight for her survival. Billions of people have taken on a one-sided attitude opposed to the Earth Cosmos. That and our general loss of centredness have so seriously interfered with the currents of the life force that it has been obvious for a long time now that there is no longer any possibility of maintaining the wonderful life that currently exists on earth's surface.

In this highly charged situation the intelligence of Earth has decided to switch over to a whole other system for her supply of energy. This is a system that was activated in the far distant past, but since has been almost completely forgotten by human beings. In consequence it has not been sympathetically affected by the devastating blockages of modern times. This alternative system draws on the sources of archetypical power that rise from the centre of the earth. In the human being, these manifest themselves in the potency of the horizontal power channels. One is located at the height of the third eye, the second at the level of the heart chakra, and the third, the most important in respect of the future supply of life force, is on the same plane as the sacrum. This last can be called the lumbar or Hara channel. The Hara channel links the storehouse of archetypical power behind our back with the sphere of manifestation located at the front of our body. It appears to lie horizontally. If one lays oneself down, the lumbar channel reveals itself as an alternative connection between heaven above us and the earth beneath. The Hara channel offers a redeeming alternative to the light channel along the spinal column.

It is amazing how the natural life around us is becoming ever more beautiful and luxuriant although nature itself is ever more clearly becoming a sacrifice to ecological destruction. This hopeful development is made possible because the elemental beings of nature are no longer dependent on the 'old' sources of life force. They are to a large extent already connected to the newly awakened 'reserve system' of life force. This is also partially true of human beings, insofar as we have recognised ourselves as being part of nature. If however we still identify strongly with the old one-dimensional space, we then remain dependent on its life forces, which are on the point of vanishing. The alternative is to open oneself to the wave of transformation, harbouring no fears about the essential alterations in our thought system and emotional attitude. Naturally, it is not a matter of losing oneself. Quite the opposite. It is rather a matter of seeking one's own centre and getting into conversation with the core of one's own soul, and thereby with the soul of creation too, which would never surrender us to a deficiency of the life force.

52.   Three Levels of Grounding

It is quite recently that the theme of grounding has needed its own chapter. It used to be self-evident that the force of gravity kept us beings of the earth's surface securely chained to the planet. Every atom of life was held in its place by the attractive power of earth's centre. One might talk poetically of the seductive power of Mother Earth that holds us clasped close to her bosom. However, for some few years past Earth has betaken herself on the unsafe road towards the transformation of her essential Being, and now much has been turned on its head. Grounding has lost its self-evident quality. There are various reasons why this is so. For example, to make possible a restructuring of living space, it is necessary to loosen the ties that hold the currents of life firmly attached to their old tracks. For sure, this leads towards Chaos, but the loss of systemic order is a necessary risk to permit the transformation of earth space.

The partial lifting of terrestrial attraction can also be understood as a needed challenge, addressed to us human beings. The stereotype of our old relationship with the earth is being put in question; even its physical basis is near vanishing point. Our multi-dimensional bodily organism is extremely sensitive in this respect. If we are not well grounded, our supply of life force is weakened. People are already beginning to worry about survival. Our organs react with critical symptoms. To survive, humanity is being required to discover new relationships with Sister Earth and to live them in as yet unanticipated ways. In addition to the force of gravity that holds us physically attached to the planet earth, one can speak of three levels of grounding. During an epoch of transformation, one should be aware of the energetic level of grounding, and also of the quality of one's soul and spiritual grounding.

The reason for this great change in the vital-energetic coordinates of grounding is that the separation between heaven and earth has lost its meaning. Since we now find ourselves in a unified and thoroughly connected Earth Cosmos, one can speak of a spherical grounding. To be anchored to the vault of heaven is just as important as being anchored to earth's centre. One should visualise that fine threads of power anchor one's personal Holon to the vault of heaven as firmly as to different points in the depths of the earth. There are two strands of thread involved, running in opposite directions. Their powers of attraction should be evenly balanced.

As regards the second level of grounding, there should be a good connection between the qualities of our soul and the power organism of our body. Traditionally, the soul presence is anchored in the mineral content of the bones and the iron particles in the blood, but because the status of the physical level is undergoing such sharp changes, the soul is now having a hard time finding sufficient stability to maintain an anchorage in the manifested world. It therefore grabs at the nearest possible means of anchoring itself in the world of matter.

One can assist the soul in this endeavour. In the region behind our back there is a hidden light channel that runs parallel to the vertebral channel. This is an organ for anchoring spirit in matter and its usual function enables the time span of our incarnation within earth's systems. Or, in reverse, the light channel behind our back allows the spirit to free itself from the chains of matter. One could call it the channel of birth and death. To ground the soul, one should lean firmly against the support of the light channel in one's back region, which can best be done lying down.

As regards the spiritual level of grounding, there is no kind of support against which a person could lean. The spiritual aspect of grounding is guaranteed to those who have made a firm decision in their hearts to serve the further evolution of earthly life. Dearest Earth, since you have already decided on your own behalf to complete the path of epochal transformation, I stand beside you ready to bring the processes of transformation to all the planes of Being.

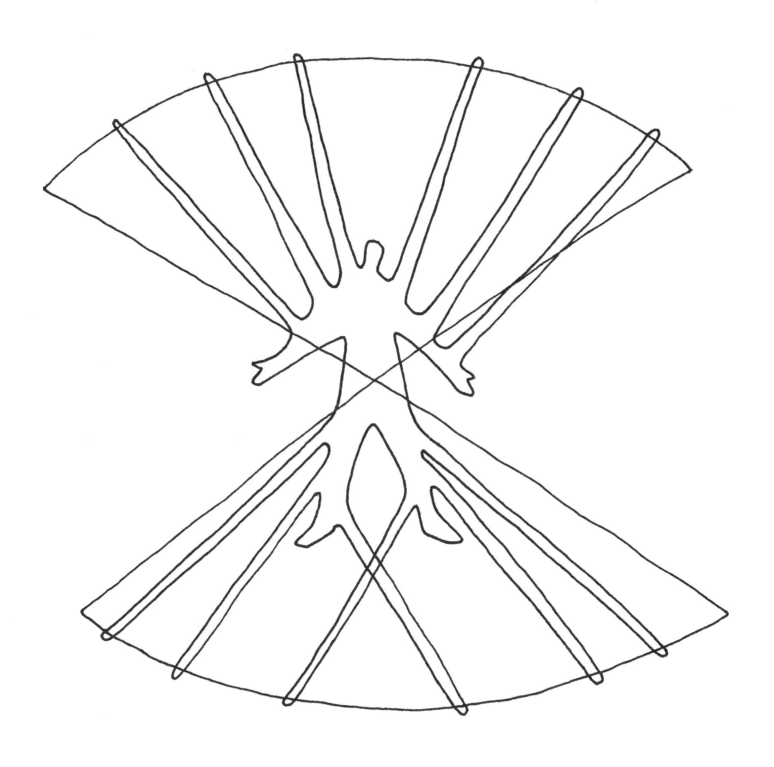

To be anchored spherically to heaven and to the depths of the earth.

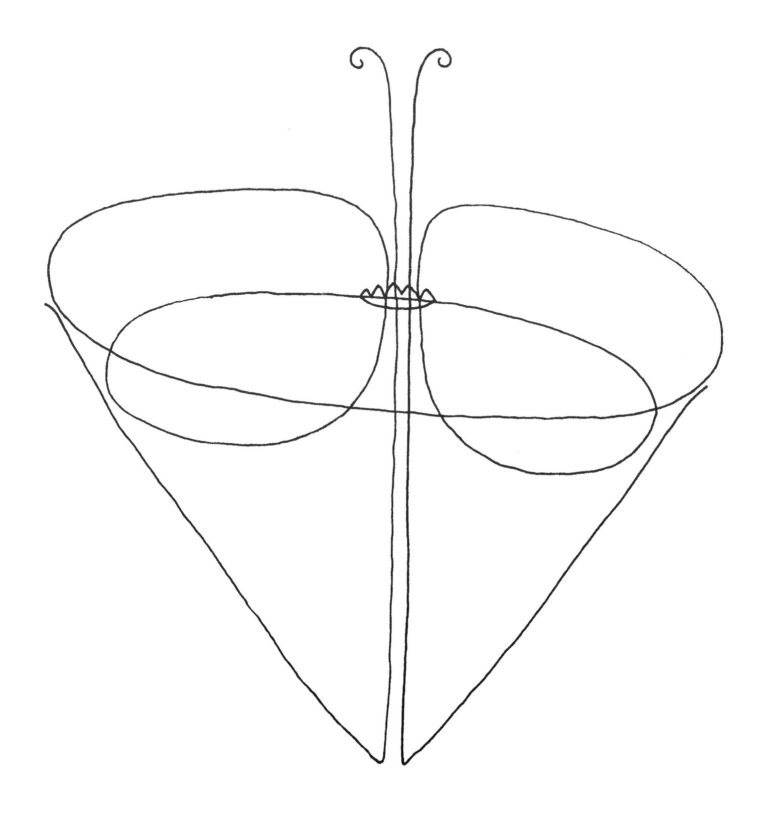

Hawaiian volcanoes in the midst of the watery mass of the Pacific Ocean.

53. Hawaii: Oceans and Mountains Work Together

Truly, the balance of earth's surface is wonderfully conceived! The tallest mountains jutting towards heaven are as high as the profoundest troughs of the Pacific Ocean are deep. The vertical pyramids of the mountains represent the planet's masculine aspect and stand for its Yang on the earth's surface. The oceans, those giant basins full of water, represent earth's feminine quality, her Yin. The feminine pole is of fundamental importance for the development of life, and, appropriately, these watery expanses cover the largest part of earth's surface.

Since we humans are not beings of the water element, we can only view the oceans from without. We know them just as broad expanses. One's imagination must do a somersault to experience the monstrous power and breathtaking grandeur of earth's feminine element. Let us imagine that the watery mass of ocean is standing upright. Towering before our astonished eyes are mighty mountain ranges composed of water. Look at the mighty mountains and lofty plateaus made of water! They shine in the sunlight like gigantic water crystals. Yet they are quite soft and transparent withal.

Like other islands in the Pacific, Hawaii lies amid giant underwater mountains, which, as regards the surrounding archipelago, rise an average of over 3000 meters from the ocean floor; the island of Hawaii itself consists of mountains that likewise stretch 3000 meters up into the sky. However, the Hawaiian archipelago is an enormous volcanic cone, and therefore we are looking at fiery formations that starkly represent the Yang pole, quite opposite to the Yin of the Pacific's watery mountain ranges amidst which it lies. In Hawaii, fire and water collide with evenly matched power. Hawaii represents the navel of the Pacific, the point of perfect balance between the feminine and masculine, between Yin and Yang.

The moment has now come that cosmic forces may round out our imaginative powers. Envision the earth's surface as a far-reaching, interdependent composition of various watery lenses – think of the watery mass of individual oceans, seas and lakes. Those huge watery lenses collect the archetypical forces of the externally oriented universe – the universe of stars, planets and galaxies. In contrast, in many places the continents have been folded into the shapes of huge masses of rock. Their mountain peaks tower like crystalline pyramids into the heights – but their primary connection is not with the stars of heaven but the cosmic forces of the inward universe of earth.

Mountain ranges and volcanic cones – like Hawaii – are nourished with the archetypical forces of Being from the earth's centre. Primarily, they embody the energies of the deeper parts of earth. The impact of cosmic forces, on the one hand through watery lenses and on the other through mountain pyramids, encourages the exchange between the inwardly and outwardly oriented universe to take place on the earth's surface. Thus life can prosper.

The navel of Hawaii plays a special role in this interaction. It has already been said that in regard to Hawaii, the gravitational and levitational forces of the Earth Cosmos are perfectly balanced. Their Yin-Yang polarisation is also extremely strong but stable, based on the balance between water and fire. The perfect balance that exists internally makes possible Hawaii's external balancing role. Its task within the paradigm of the Holon of the Pacific Ocean is to balance the Ocean's near-endlessly expansive space and preserve its tranquillity.

Oceans are the guardians of peace and calm on the earth's surface. Their own surface is sometimes churned up by storms but the stillness of their depths remains untroubled. The role played by Hawaii empowers the calm of the Pacific Ocean. The communicating column between the inner and outer universe, maintained and stabilised by the archipelago, is made into an anchor of peace. It is through this 'anchor of peace' that the calm of the Pacific Ocean is held fast in the unimaginable depths of the ocean that lie below the ocean. This last is the ocean of the Earth Soul's emotional power on which swims the membrane that we call the earth's surface. One can liken the ocean below the ocean to the loving power of Mother and Sister Earth.

Exercise 41, to experience the forces of the Hara channel

Imagine that a ball of light, as big as will fit, is lying between your hips.

Now spend some time rocking your pelvis back and forth.

In so doing, do not move the ball but hold it in place.

In a single instant, abruptly break off the rocking motion. As you do so, watch the ball of light ascend.

When the ball has reached the heart space, pay attention to the vibrations that it has carried up with it. What is their quality? What sort of power do they bring to the light of day?

Now let them radiate into the world.

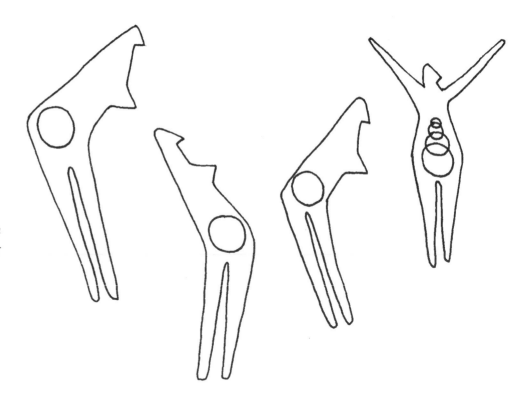

Exercise 42, for the threefold grounding

Stand upright. Imagine that, through different points on the soles of your feet, your entire body is anchored deep in the earth's centre. (We are dealing here with the energetic aspect of grounding).

After a short while, transfer to the soul aspect of grounding.

Imagine that your soul is standing on your knees. Let the feeling of her presence slide downwards till it has touched the earth beneath your feet.

Finally, there follows the spiritual grounding.

Imagine that a corner of heaven descends down through your body, right to the tip of your tailbone.

Next, take the focus of your concentration to a deeper level, as far as the chakra of the earth element located between your knees.

Energetic Drawing 21

A cluster of violets radiates their life force, and behind them is their deva, guardian of the archetype of the violet genus.

Humanity has lost its conscious relationship with the intelligence of earth, and in consequence retains no memory of the evolution of elemental beings. Commonly one speaks of three evolutionary strands that use the advantages of earth's surface for their further development. Plants, animals and human beings have a physical body and so are visible to the intellect. Their existence cannot be denied. In contrast, elemental beings are not embodied in matter at all, but should be regarded as an evolution of consciousness.

As a manifestation of the thoughts and feelings of the Earth Soul, they can have no bodies composed of muscle and bone. Their task is to take the inspirations of Gaia and incorporate them in the landscape and the different creatures of her surface, and convey the Earth Soul's ministrations to them so that they may prosper to the maximum extent.

The form of elemental beings corresponds to a definite procedure that the collective consciousness of earth has developed in order to accompany and guide the evolution of the landscape, plants, animals and humans that occupy earth's surface. In the first place, one should visualise the elemental being as a defined power structure. It is the bearer of an independent intelligence that can perceive the Earth Soul's current assignment and transfer it to the appropriate living creature. Elemental beings are simultaneously both messengers of the Earth Soul and technicians of her biosphere. The traditions of different cultures tell of nymphs and fairies, dwarves and salamanders, devas and other invisible beings that ensoul the nature kingdoms. The diversity of their forms of appearance corresponds to the diversity of living creatures and the multidimensionality of the phenomena on earth's crust. All must be cared for and protected in the way that is appropriate to them. Elemental beings are the wonderful and highly specialised attendants that care for humans, animals, plants, minerals and landscapes.

The present epoch of transformation has brought a degree of turmoil into the evolution of elemental beings. The Earth Soul has generated new kinds of elemental beings to enable her to accompany the development of earth's new ecosphere. The classical elemental beings recognise a clearly defined system through which they perform their service within the framework of the four elements. Beings of the water element are responsible for the development of life processes. Beings of the earth element are masters of form and are active wherever life is shaped or maintained in a particular form. Beings of fire are agents of change. Their desire is to connect each ending with a new beginning. Beings of the air element are primarily concerned with the coordination of the life processes within the space of a particular landscape.

The 'new' elemental beings know no such sort of specialization. They act as beings of the fifth element, the ether element that has the power to combine all four elements. One can speak of the beings of the ether element in the following sense: their task is to work on the construction of an integrated, holistic space within whose framework different planes and dimensions connect with each other. They can best be recognised by their proficiency in communication. Elemental beings of the ether element no longer exhibit any fear of human beings. On the contrary, based on the holistic nature of their consciousness, they feel themselves to be on a par with humans. They long to cooperate with us on the construction of the new earth space.

The Earth Consciousness is also in the process of developing a further kind of elemental being, one that would be ready to help humans to find the right path in the labyrinth of the approaching transformations. The issue revolves particularly around the changes in bodily structures and functions that will come upon us during the processes of our harmonisation with earth's new ecosphere. This kind of elemental being is often encountered in the parks of great cities, the sort of park where many people go daily about their business. Such parks are the meeting places for the two evolutionary strands – human and elemental – that until now have been kept severely apart. It is now up to us to fashion the future together. One can recognise this particular kind of elemental being by their command of human emotional language. They are capable of imparting the Earth Soul's love and care for those of us who shy away from the approaching transformation.

55. Veneration of the Pure Heart

In a globalised world that is dependent on the constant exchange of material and intellectual capital, people feel forced to be constantly active. We work and work and still don't have enough time to accomplish even more. Naturally, one can withdraw from the pressure of such busy-ness. But therein lurks another danger. It is very easy to come under the influence of the ideological mechanisms. It does not matter what sort of face they wear, religious, intellectual or political. They always demand that we humans perform specific rituals, spiritual practices or organisational duties. One is constantly called upon to carry out this or that project... It cannot be wrong to feel oneself impelled to be active. It becomes questionable if, in doing so, a person loses, in each passing instant, the sense of the presence of eternity. The cult of continual activity, even when dedicated to good ends, can be devastating. It jeopardises the Earth Cosmos' fundamental balance based on the rhythm of a constant alternation between activity and times of rest, between the service devoted to daily life and quiet reverence for the divine.

Take care! The intellect is smart enough to arrange for reverential time among the activities initiated by its imperial power. Prayer times are prescribed; idols and spiritual masters are deployed as objects of veneration. Lest the pilgrims forget why they had journeyed to the sacred place, objects of devotion are produced non-stop and put on sale so that the vending booths buckle under their weight.

Reverence must be better understood. It needs neither to be led nor pointed towards the highest goal. The sense of hierarchy, that there is always someone above us to whom we owe the highest respect and is worthy of our veneration, is a long time past its due date. True veneration is a form of self-knowledge of the divine nature of the Whole that is manifested in every individual event and in every moment. Veneration is not a linear effort directed towards a particular goal. It is matter of spherical intuition, a feeling that spreads out to all sides from the heart of the reverent person, and so grounds itself in the conscious Being of its own wellspring. The veneration of the pure heart expresses itself through a language that is used by angels, mountains, lakes and stars, a language that is the direct experience of the divine presence. What is the grammar of such a language? It is very simple: one radiates in one's wholeness from one's heart centre, whereby one can simultaneously be grateful as much for one's existence as for one's ability to radiate from the centre of one's own being. Forgiveness, Faith and Being are equivalent forms of veneration. Also, the veneration of the pure heart is like a silent prayer.

Why should it be important, in this epoch of transformation, to remind oneself of the power of veneration? In the first place, it is an excellent tool for withdrawing oneself from the dominion of the egocentric consciousness. If one is ready to open oneself to the flame of veneration, that instantly lets all the air out of the puffed-up ego. Borne by the power of the soul, the veneration of the pure heart can be a healing force in every situation. In the second place, many people worldwide do not realize their responsibility for life, and consequently the planet's emotional fields are being poisoned wholesale by feelings of fear, envy, hostility, etc. This cripples her (the planet) in fundamental ways, obstructing the circulation of the transformative forces. Essentially, it prevents Earth's self-healing process from operating.

At such a time, it makes sense to let the sound of prayer ring out. If, at some critical moment, individual persons and groups were to build the field of veneration of the pure heart, the vibrational quality of earth space would be raised so high that a redemptive movement could be unleashed. Veneration of the pure heart means that there are no motives to inspire one to give oneself to silent prayer, other than the wish to take part in the constant veneration of the universal Being. Actually, one should learn to take part in that whatever the moment and whatever one is doing.

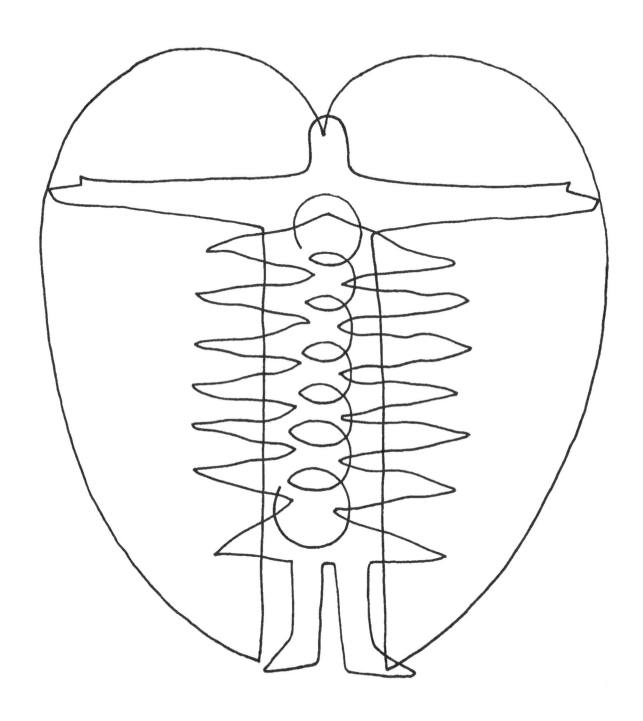

When the flames of the veneration of the pure heart illuminate the human being.

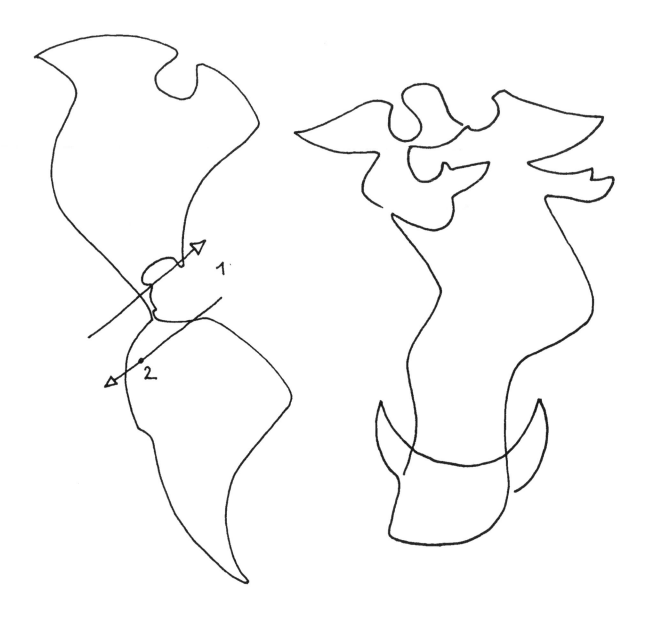

The winged 'Virgin of Quito', personification of the Earth Soul, in relation to the two aspects of the American continent.

1 = inter-oceanic power channels, 2 = the location of Quito

56. Quito, Ecuador: America and the Earth Soul

One can see at a glance that the American continent is composed of two strongly polarized parts that are held together by the umbilical cord of Central America. North America becomes ever broader as it approaches earth's North Pole. In contrast, South America becomes ever thinner towards the South Pole. Seen from the standpoint of Central America, the southern part of the continent ends in a regularly tapered point while the northern part runs contrarily, taking the form of a broad front reminiscent of two wings. If one regards the earth's surface as a Holon, one can propose that every continent and every ocean plays a specific role in its organism. One may ask, if Africa stands for the life force of earth, Asia for her creative forces, Australia for her archetypical quality, Europe for her consciousness, what would be America's role? I suggest that America stands for the soul quality of the Earth Cosmos.

The two poles of the American continent represent two aspects of the Earth Soul. The task for North America is to bring the spiritual forces of the Earth Soul to expression on the planet's surface. This is why the continent's northern part exhibits Yang traits. In contrast, South America embodies a feminine (Yin) character and represents the Earth Soul's emotional forces. Together the spiritual and emotional aspects of the Earth Soul form a unity. The role of the dragon's back of the Rocky Mountains, extended by the Andes, is to demonstrate that the two parts of the continent belong with each other. The role played by the two oceans that together embrace America is no less important in ensuring the balance of the Earth Soul's Yang and Yin aspects. They too are polarised, the one opposite to the other. The Atlantic Ocean tends to concentrate its energy in a line that runs midmost between the coasts of America and Africa. The Atlantic shows a Yang character in balance to the Yin quality of the Pacific Ocean, which the latter's rounded expanse reveals.

The two oceans approach very close to each other in Central America, the same region where the spiritual and emotional aspects of the Earth Soul also come to meet each other. Both oceans communicate with each other in the same area, but not through the Panama Canal! The Pacific and Atlantic Oceans exchange their forces through two power channels that run through the atmosphere of Central America. The northernmost touches Yucatan and Florida, the southern one crosses Ecuador and the island of Puerto Rico. The northern light channel carries Yin forces towards the Atlantic while the Yang forces flow towards the Pacific through the southern channel. Quito, the capital of Ecuador, was built in a 3000-meter high valley in the midst of the Andes. The city's axis points along the southern power channel that ties the Atlantic to the Pacific Ocean. We may presume that in pre-Columbian times the city's axis originally followed a ritual path laid in accordance with the axis of the inter-oceanic light channel. Their sacred mountains, such as Atacazo and Imbabura, lie along the same axis, as does the extensive complex of pyramids called Cochasqui, to the north of Quito.

Today, the hill held to be holiest along this axis is located in the middle of the city. In form it resembles a step pyramid. The Spaniards have jestingly called it 'el panecillo' (the loaf of bread). However, the Indians have named it after its true function in the landscape: 'Shungoloma', the hill of the heart. There within it pulsates the heart of the Andes. Nowadays Shungoloma is crowned by a gigantic statue of the Virgin Mary, who presides over the city. This is a copy of the 'Virgin of Quito' that Bernardo de Legardo sculpted in the year 1734. It is unique in that not only does she stand on the moon, but she also has wings. The moon, connected with the rhythms of watery expanses, can be seen as a symbol of the emotional aspect of the Earth Soul, which South America represents. However, the wings reveal that the Virgin of Quito is also an incarnation of the Earth Soul's spiritual aspect, which expresses itself through North America. In the Virgin of Quito the two aspects of the American continent are unified.

Exercise 43, to experience two levels of the elemental world

Seek out a flower that is blooming.

Bend down to the flower you have selected and look at it attentively and lovingly.

At a specific instant, slip into the flower, as a bee does when it is gathering honey.

At the same instant, look around you and sense the quality of a flower's interior space, how it feels to you. Be aware that you are now on the plane of elemental beings. In the case of flowers, it is the fairy realm, because fairy consciousness is responsible for the colour quality of the blooms.

Immediately afterwards (in your imagination), make a forward somersault, so that you find yourself on a higher plane. This is the plane of the archetypical consciousness of the kind of flower you selected, the world of the devas.

After this, you should once again become conscious of the flower and its outward beauty, and in the process be swept back into awareness of everyday life.

The exercise should be performed with several different types of flower to help you practice the power of discrimination.

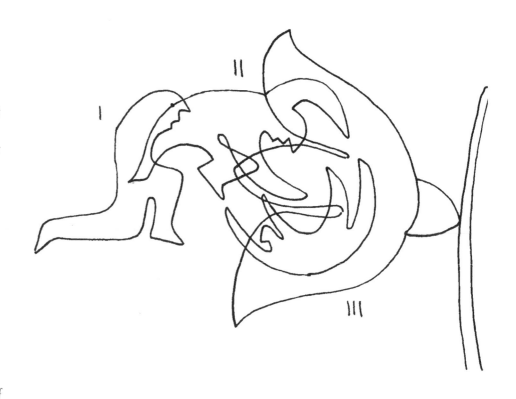

Exercise 44, to master the culture of the heart – the veneration of the pure heart – and realize it in daily life

Seven principles of the heart culture are necessary to its realization.

So that you can experience their individual qualities, they are juxtaposed with the seven chakras that vibrate along your spinal column.

To stimulate the intensity of the experience, you should apply the colours of the seven chakras, so that the corresponding colour radiates in your heart centre.

The following are the seven principles of veneration:

1. *Pure heart forgiving (Ruby Red)*
2. *Pure heart living (Orange)*
3. *Pure heart decision-making (Yellow)*
4. *Pure heart loving (Green)*
5. *Pure heart creating (Blue)*
6. *Pure heart seeing (Violet)*
7. *Pure heart venerating (White)*

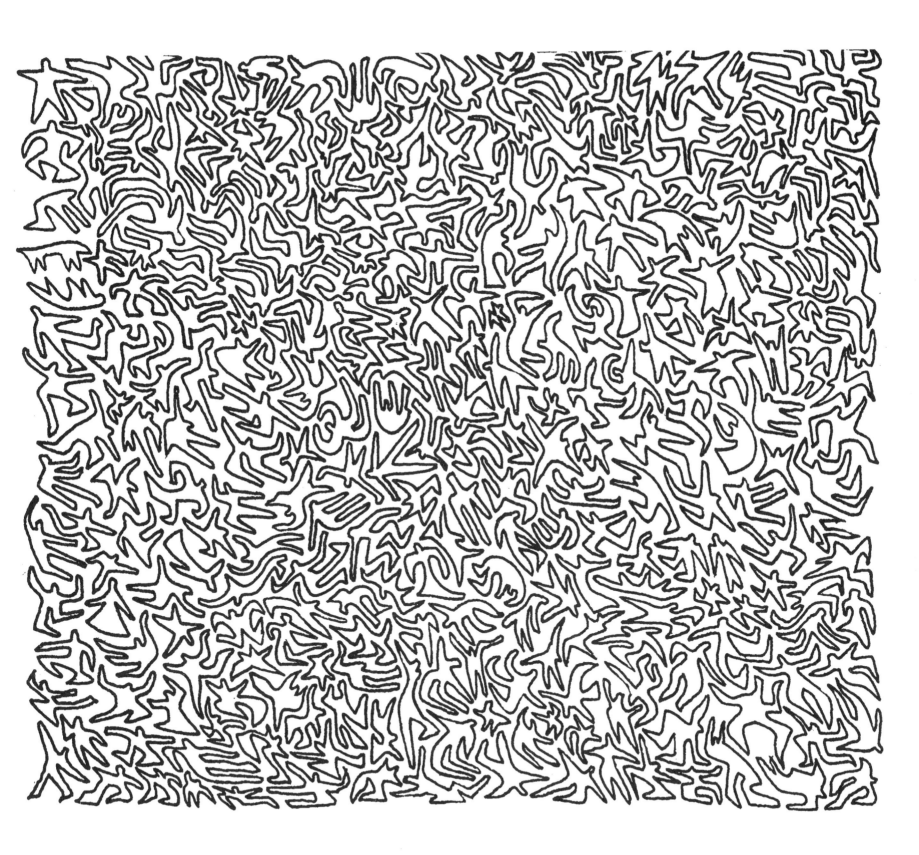

Energetic Drawing 22

Earth's self-healing process means that the Earth Soul has decided to intervene in the activities on the earth's surface.

57. Dearest Earth, How Are You Doing?

The concept of earth healing was originally unveiled as a criticism of the anthropocentric attitude of modern spiritual movements. Methods to heal and harmonise the human body and our psychological condition are continuously being developed, but in so doing we humans often forget that we are only a part of a much more complex organism and consciousness, one that we call earth. To get to grips with the situation, we try to open ourselves to the problems that our present civilization is causing within the terrestrial organism. We look first at the blockages and disharmonies that arise continually as our civilization spreads wide over the earth's surface without any awareness of the vital-energetic, emotional or spiritual extensions of earth space; secondly, we look at the traumas that occur because people and states have been fighting each other for thousands of years and plunging each other into misery and misfortune. The resulting traumas work back from the memory of the individual places and landscapes into the current streams of life, which does not allow world peace to prosper.

These are the reasons why, parallel to the development of science-based ecology, there has been an attempt to develop different methods to heal the invisible wounds from which our sister earth is suffering, and to implement them. Such methods show themselves to be more artistic than scientific. This is in order that they may address in a correct manner the sensitivity of the planes of the ecosphere that are at issue. One thinks of lithopuncture (earth acupuncture), healing through sound, colour images, dance, etc. Nonetheless, the same causes that impel earth's destruction are constantly being repeated, and possibly even reinforced. Sooner or later it becomes obvious that the entire earth healing effort makes no sense unless contemporary attitudes regarding the Earth Cosmos are fundamentally transformed.

To establish a thought system that ratifies the holistic perception of the terrestrial ecosphere, the old concept of geomancy was taken up and defined anew. In contrast to geology, geomancy concerns itself with the exploration of the invisible as well as the visible planes of earth's totality. In the structure of a geomantic investigation, the intellectual, emotional, and vital-energetic dimensions of a place are as worthy of notice as its materialised forms. Further, the mind-set of modern geomancy in no way separates human development, including our self-regarding consciousness, from the pulsations of earth's wholeness. If we are talking about healing the earth, we are thinking primarily of the transformation of the people who have recognised that their defective relationship with their own wholeness and the Earth Cosmos screams out to heaven for redress. If one addresses the consequences of this defective relationship, the healing process within the earth's ecosphere can actually happen. It is really the earth's self-healing processes that make it possible for us humans to gradually become ready to take over the responsibility for our destructive activities on the earth's surface.

Parallel to this comes the realisation that even the unhealthy activities within earth space are an important component of earth's self-healing process. The destructive clamour of the elements, manifest in floods, volcanic eruptions, storms, etc., and the ravages of death-dealing diseases too, are not to be viewed only as negative developments. On the one hand they hasten the dissolution of obsolete projections regarding the character both of earth and humans that hinder our civilization's development of a holistic way of life. On the other hand they help dissolve the old, antiquated arrangement of space that holds the earth-organism, and human consciousness too, prisoners in the linear structure of a rationalistically conceived reality. The shift appears to be in the direction of chaotic living conditions, a prospect from which we humans shy away. Actually, the issue is one of transformation, without which the dissolution of the obsolete structures would be impossible. In order not to become the victim of global fears, one should pay attention to the phenomena of the new earth space. They stand witness that earth's self-healing process is already well advanced.

58. Challenge 2012:
59 Foundation Stones of a Peaceful Civilization

When the year 1999 passed into 2000 without leaving any notable waymark behind it, we shifted our concentration to the next threshold, 2012. This year marks the end of the celebrated Mayan calendar. Was that date, 2012, foreseen to be the end of time? It is true that a sinister activity, a process of transformation, is ongoing within the wholeness of earth. Nor can it be denied that time is running out; our space is barely capable of sustaining our grossly overstretched civilization. There is a feeling that more and more problems are accumulating within us and around us, and yet the time available to solve them is growing less and less. Confronted by all the unresolved problems that our civilization is daily creating, how can we avoid triggering a worldwide wave of fear?

In the first place, no one should lose their sense of inner peace. Nothing can happen that we ourselves have not helped to shape. No event can come upon us that we have not loosed upon ourselves. No cosmic deadline (the year 2012 for example) can be settled in advance without destroying our freedom, the divine favour that has been given us. Secondly, to avoid the collapse of civilization, we must maintain a clear vision of what we are and what quality of life we look for as our daily reality. If such a vision exists among us, the forces that guide the transformation process will find in us a partner with whose help they can push aside the hurdles that stand in the way of planetary transformation. On the etheric planes one can trace the challenge that faces us humans: it is to imagine a clear path for our further evolution and carry it in our hearts as hope.

There is not much more that needs to be said. This book, Touching the Breath of Gaia, already speaks to 59 aspects of a holistic planetary culture. This culture is oriented towards more than mere materialism and it no longer places the divine exclusively on the spiritual plane. It is a culture that looks at the life in us and around us with multidimensional eyes and pays attention to all possible aspects of the living reality. There is not one that shall be overlooked or disdained.

From this derives the trinity of this future and yet already conceptually existing civilization of the Earth Cosmos. Fundamental to this trinity is the inner development of every individual person as a co-creator of the new culture. This means that each person learns to reawaken their own sensibility, to follow their cycles of transformation and personally to embody the power of love. Unconditionally appertaining is to maintain one's inner peace and pay attention to the voice of the soul (the inner 'I'); also to be ready to talk to others and serve the evolution of earth's ecosphere.

The second branch of the trinity of this envisaged civilization is concerned with relationships within society. The economic system, for example, is regarded as a creative opportunity through which people can exchange their abilities and pieces of information. Religion will be honoured as a path to the universal conjointness of each individual. Art will be seen as source of a creative language through which the different worlds and dimensions can communicate with each other. The democratic political system includes not only humans but also all other beings of the earthly cosmos. One can speak of pan-democracy.

The third branch of the new culture embodies human social relationships with the other worlds of the earth cosmos. This is not just a matter of relations with the plant and animal worlds but also human relations with the elemental beings who, on earth's surface, are the embodiment of her Soul. They are the masters of harmonious technology. Linked thereto is geomancy, as an ecological tool through which to comprehend the multidimensionality of the landscape. Not to be overlooked is the relationship with the angelic world, which represents the consciousness of the universe. Incarnate humanity's co-creative relationships with the world of ancestors and descendants also have important significance. Considering the external circumstances now existing on the earth's surface, one may get the impression that this outline of a peaceful civilization is quite utopian. But one should ask what one's heart has to say about it.

The Earth Soul has laid an egg. When comes the decisive moment that it will break through its shell?

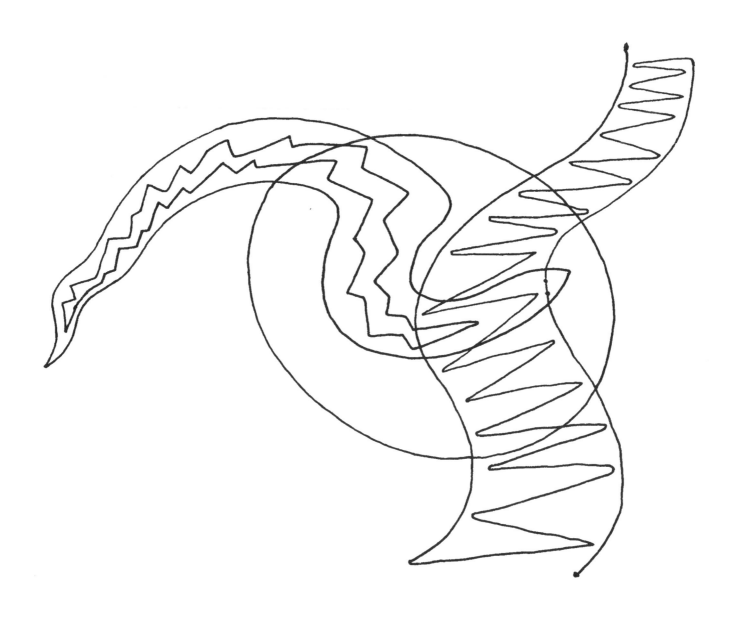

The watery and the fiery dragons encounter each other in the Rio de Janeiro area.

59. Rio de Janeiro:
In Conversation with the Atlantic Ocean

The name Rio de Janeiro suggests a great river, which the discoverers suspected existed. There is no such 'rio' on the physical plane. However, there is a huge etheric river in the area, and it flows in a direction opposite to what is expected of a river. It is a river of watery ether that finds its source in the depths of the Atlantic Ocean and flows toward the South American continent. On the continent's coast, in the middle of Rio de Janeiro, this invisible river rises onto firm ground and flows inland. Because of this mighty stream one can say that the ocean and continent communicate with each other in the area of Rio de Janeiro. The exchange between the archetypical powers of ocean and the landscapes of South America begins amid the cityscape of Rio de Janeiro.

One can imagine a stream of watery ether being woven together out of many different power currents in the expanses of the ocean. This broad stream reaches the American coast in the area of Rio's best-known beach, called Copacabana. To the inner sight, the etheric stream looks like a watery dragon that winds its way through Rio's cityscape towards the northwest. The particular strength of Rio's space arises because, in the middle of the city, the 'watery dragon' of ocean collides with a 'fiery dragon' emanating from the mountain chain of the Serra de Carioca whose shape resembles a dragon. These mountains draw their power from the fiery nature of the granite of which their geological body is composed. The conflict between the polarized currents of watery and fiery ether creates a strong force field in the middle of Rio. This circular force field houses a definitive chakra of the South American continent. It is centred in the granite mountain of Corcovado, which is characterised by the tall Christ figure with outstretched arms.

The chakra of Rio de Janeiro can be compared with the human root chakra. The terrestrial root chakra acts as a power centre through which the archetypical forces of the earth's centre are drawn up to the surface of the continent. At the same time the life forces of the earth's surface are anchored in the 'ocean' of archetypical power located at the earth's centre. The power of Rio's root chakra is drawn out of the earth's depths from two strong power sources. One is located on the edge of a large sweet water lake called the Lagoa. It is largely blocked by the urban structures of the Leblon town district. Not much better are the circumstances of the second spring, located near the celebrated Church of our Lady of the Glory of the Outeiro. This church is a magnificent piece of 18th century architecture. It stands on the last foothill of the Serra de Carioca, which once was washed by the waves of ocean. The power source belonging to it was then deep underwater. In the 1960s the immediate area was quite shattered by the construction of a motorway that was driven past the Church of the Glory. The consequent turmoil has obstructed the power source to a significant degree.

In the Rio de Janeiro area there are also individual granite mountains that are part of the composition of the root chakra. They rise up as if grown from the ground, like gigantic megaliths. Their probable function in the root chakra realm is to bring forth the spiritual and emotional qualities of the earth's centre – meaning the Earth Soul – into the light of day. The most famous of these mountains is the 'Sugarloaf' – Pao de Acucar. In its shape and message it resembles an egg. We are looking here at the archetype of the original World Egg within which the whole earthly creation slumbers like a seed before it is awakened and made manifest. The area's most mysterious megalith however is the Pedra de Gavea. Its peak resembles two godlike faces that are wearing a hat and looking in opposite directions. The task of the mountain-like megalith of Pedra de Gavea is to embody the presence of the Earth Soul, which is in communication with the different extensions of the universe. To enable this sacred role to be maintained aright, a mighty heart centre has become manifest at its foot and sends its beams out over land and ocean.

Exercise 45, to overcome the constrictive power of rationality

Take a few moments of your valuable time for yourself. Breathe in and out a few times to relax.

Imagine that your head is a ball of light. You should actually, in virtual reality, convert your head into a light-filled ball.

After this, imagine that you grip the ball with both hands and carefully carry it down into your heart region.

Keep the ball in the centre of your heart space (in the centre of your breast) till it becomes as light as a soap bubble.

Then the ball will rise up of its own accord and once again unite with your physical head.

Give thanks, and from now on trust your multi-layered intelligence.

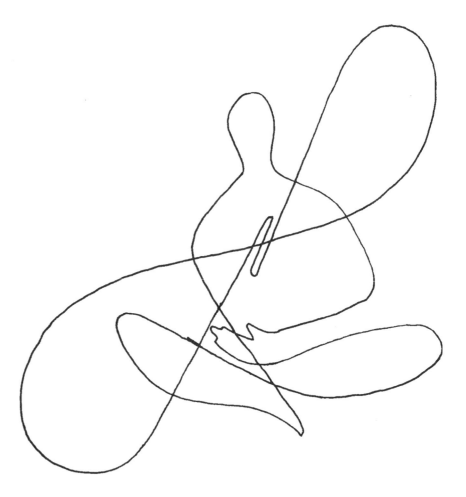

Exercise 46, to experience the new quality of earth space

This exercise relates to the mystery of the 'eye of the needle.' The 'eye of the needle' represents the passage from one state of consciousness to another, which is conditional on transformation.

Imagine that you see the thin interstice of the eye of the needle in your heart centre. It is just as important to sense it as to visualise it.

As you inhale, draw the space in front of you back through the needle's eye towards your backspace. You should breathe with your lips lightly pressed together so that you can hear the breath passing over them.

As you exhale, draw the backspace forward and out to the front of you through the needle's eye.

Repeat this type of breathing several times. By so doing, one opens oneself to perceive the new quality that has meantime been building.

One can also breathe in the same way through the needle's eye of the other five chakras that pulsate between the crown and root chakras.

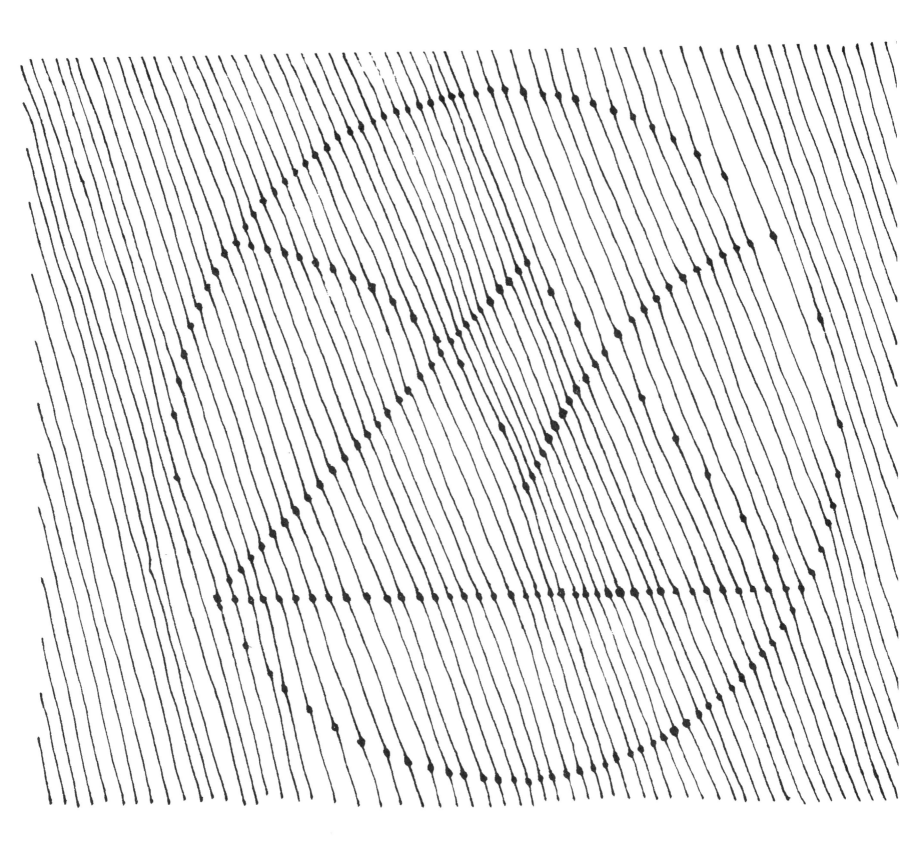

Energetic Drawing 23

Postscript

Yesterday I returned from the Philippines, having experienced the third super-typhoon to strike the country during 2006. Such disastrous tempests, capable of knocking out a whole country, were unknown to previous generations.

On the flight home I saw the film, which is being shown worldwide, about the far-reaching impacts of ongoing global warming. This film, *The Unpleasant Truth*, was created by Al Gore, former Vice-President of the United States. I had just experienced in the Philippines the reality of its message: humanity and Earth are right now facing a most challenging ecological crisis, but we are still trying to avoid the obvious facts.

I respect and do my best to follow the proposals given at the end of the film on ways to avoid the cataclysm. These refer to 'personal ecology', as it is called: i.e., change your own mental attitudes, your way of dealing with modern technologies, your personal relationship to the environment...

Through the present book I hope to transmit to my fellow human beings my inspiration regarding a complementary issue – the opening of conscious conversation and collaboration with Gaia. This entails a series of enabling steps:

1. Stop pretending that the Earth is a nobody. The Earth is a gigantic creative and immensely wise consciousness. Now is the ultimate chance to acknowledge her capacity to communicate. Let us talk to her about the measures that she, Gaia, mother of creation, has developed and already set in motion to avoid ecological disaster. Let us start collaborating with her 'emergency plan'.

2. *Touch the Breath of Gaia!* Learn the language that is familiar to her and to the holographic units of her consciousness, spirits and other beings of our environment. The exercises listed in this book give us the opportunity to dive into the grammar of this universal language. She is already using this language to talk to us through our bodies, imaginations, and intuitions.

3. The time is ripe for us to express the love and adoration we feel for Gaia without people laughing at us. Let us go further: let us tell her about the kind of peaceful civilisation that we would like to establish upon the Earth and ask for her support and guidance to ensure the success of our heartfelt intentions.

Marko Pogačnik
Sempas, December 3rd, 2006

FINDHORN PRESS

Books, Card Sets,
CDs & DVDs
that inspire and uplift

For a complete catalogue, please contact:

Findhorn Press Ltd
305a The Park
Forres IV36 3TE
Scotland, UK

Telephone
+44-(0)1309-690582
Fax
+44-(0)1309-690036
eMail
info@findhornpress.com

or consult our catalogue online
(with secure order facility) on
www.findhornpress.com